# White Collar Crime

# Other Books of Related Interest

## Opposing Viewpoints Series

Global Trade and Supply Chain
Human Trafficking
Poverty, Prosperity, and the Minimum Wage

## At Issue Series

Is America a Democracy or an Oligarchy?
Money Laundering
Political Corruption

## Current Controversies Series

Big Tech and Democracy
The Business of College Sports: Who Earns What
Domestic vs. Offshore Manufacturing

> "Congress shall make no law … abridging the freedom of speech, or of the press."
>
> *First Amendment to the U.S. Constitution*

The basic foundation of our democracy is the First Amendment guarantee of freedom of expression. The Opposing Viewpoints series is dedicated to the concept of this basic freedom and the idea that it is more important to practice it than to enshrine it.

# White Collar Crime

**Andrew Karpan, Book Editor**

Published in 2023 by Greenhaven Publishing, LLC
2544 Clinton Street, Buffalo NY 14224



First Edition



Articles in Greenhaven Publishing anthologies are often edited for length to meet page requirements. In addition, original titles of these works are changed to clearly present the main thesis and to explicitly indicate the author's opinion. Every effort is made to ensure that Greenhaven Publishing accurately reflects the original intent of the authors. Every effort has been made to trace the owners of the copyrighted material.

Cover image: Billion Photos/Shutterstock.com.

**Library of Congress CataloginginPublication Data**

Names: Karpan, Andrew, editor.
Title: White collar crime / Andrew Karpan, book editor.
Description: Buffalo, NY : Greenhaven Publishing, 2023. | Series: Opposing viewpoints | Includes bibliographical references and index.
Identifiers: LCCN 2022056736 | ISBN 9781534509269 (library binding) | ISBN 9781534509252 (paperback)
Subjects: LCSH: White collar crimes--Law and legislation--United States--Juvenile literature. | Bribery--Law and legislation--United States--Juvenile literature. | Money laundering--Law and legislation--United States--Juvenile literature. | Trade secrets--Law and legislation--United States--Criminal provisions--Juvenile literature. | Investments--Law and legislation--United States--Criminal provisions--Juvenile literature.
Classification: LCC KF9350 .W4275 2023 | DDC 345.73/0268--dc23/eng/20230105
LC record available at https://lccn.loc.gov/2022056736

*Manufactured in the United States of America*

Website: http://greenhavenpublishing.com

# Contents

## Chapter 3: Can Trade Secrets Be Stolen?



## Chapter 4: What Makes Some Investments Illegal?

# The Importance of Opposing Viewpoints

Perhaps every generation experiences a period in time in which the populace seems especially polarized, starkly divided on the important issues of the day and gravitating toward the far ends of the political spectrum and away from a consensus-facilitating middle ground. The world that today's students are growing up in and that they will soon enter into as active and engaged citizens is deeply fragmented in just this way. Issues relating to terrorism, immigration, women's rights, minority rights, race relations, health care, taxation, wealth and poverty, the environment, policing, military intervention, the proper role of government—in some ways, perennial issues that are freshly and uniquely urgent and vital with each new generation—are currently roiling the world.

If we are to foster a knowledgeable, responsible, active, and engaged citizenry among today's youth, we must provide them with the intellectual, interpretive, and critical-thinking tools and experience necessary to make sense of the world around them and of the all-important debates and arguments that inform it. After all, the outcome of these debates will in large measure determine the future course, prospects, and outcomes of the world and its peoples, particularly its youth. If they are to become successful members of society and productive and informed citizens, students need to learn how to evaluate the strengths and weaknesses of someone else's arguments, how to sift fact from opinion and fallacy, and how to test the relative merits and validity of their own opinions against the known facts and the best possible available information. The landmark series Opposing Viewpoints has been providing students with just such critical-thinking skills and exposure to the debates surrounding society's most urgent contemporary issues for many years, and it continues to serve this essential role with undiminished commitment, care, and rigor.

The key to the series's success in achieving its goal of sharpening students' critical-thinking and analytic skills resides in its title—

Opposing Viewpoints. In every intriguing, compelling, and engaging volume of this series, readers are presented with the widest possible spectrum of distinct viewpoints, expert opinions, and informed argumentation and commentary, supplied by some of today's leading academics, thinkers, analysts, politicians, policy makers, economists, activists, change agents, and advocates. Every opinion and argument anthologized here is presented objectively and accorded respect. There is no editorializing in any introductory text or in the arrangement and order of the pieces. No piece is included as a "straw man," an easy ideological target for cheap point-scoring. As wide and inclusive a range of viewpoints as possible is offered, with no privileging of one particular political ideology or cultural perspective over another. It is left to each individual reader to evaluate the relative merits of each argument—as he or she sees it, and with the use of ever-growing critical-thinking skills—and grapple with his or her own assumptions, beliefs, and perspectives to determine how convincing or successful any given argument is and how the reader's own stance on the issue may be modified or altered in response to it.

This process is facilitated and supported by volume, chapter, and selection introductions that provide readers with the essential context they need to begin engaging with the spotlighted issues, with the debates surrounding them, and with their own perhaps shifting or nascent opinions on them. In addition, guided reading and discussion questions encourage readers to determine the authors' point of view and purpose, interrogate and analyze the various arguments and their rhetoric and structure, evaluate the arguments' strengths and weaknesses, test their claims against available facts and evidence, judge the validity of the reasoning, and bring into clearer, sharper focus the reader's own beliefs and conclusions and how they may differ from or align with those in the collection or those of their classmates.

Research has shown that reading comprehension skills improve dramatically when students are provided with compelling, intriguing, and relevant "discussable" texts. The subject matter of these collections could not be more compelling, intriguing, or urgently relevant to today's students and the world they are poised to inherit. The anthologized articles and the reading and discussion questions that are included with them also provide the basis for stimulating, lively, and passionate classroom debates. Students who are compelled to anticipate objections to their own argument and identify the flaws in those of an opponent read more carefully, think more critically, and steep themselves in relevant context, facts, and information more thoroughly. In short, using discussable text of the kind provided by every single volume in the Opposing Viewpoints series encourages close reading, facilitates reading comprehension, fosters research, strengthens critical thinking, and greatly enlivens and energizes classroom discussion and participation. The entire learning process is deepened, extended, and strengthened.

For all of these reasons, Opposing Viewpoints continues to be exactly the right resource at exactly the right time—when we most need to provide readers with the critical-thinking tools and skills that will not only serve them well in school but also in their careers and their daily lives as decision-making family members, community members, and citizens. This series encourages respectful engagement with and analysis of opposing viewpoints and fosters a resulting increase in the strength and rigor of one's own opinions and stances. As such, it helps make readers "future ready," and that readiness will pay rich dividends for the readers themselves, for the citizenry, for our society, and for the world at large.

# Introduction

> *"It is time the nation woke up and realized that it's not the armed robbers or drug dealers who cause the most economic harm, it's the white collar criminals living in the most expensive homes who have the most impressive resumes who harm us the most."*
>
> *–Harry Markopolos, American forensic accounting and forensic fraud investigator*

The idea of what is legal and what is not is a major part of how society is organized and how it sees itself. What is illegal sits outside the organized world and reflects the polar opposite of the values that it holds dear. Theft, violence, avarice, greed. By their very logic, laws seek to contain those negative characteristics and put them outside the realm of civil society. But nevertheless, the same crimes constantly reappear and are constantly punished, imparting the same lessons ad infinitum.

But as society has gotten more complicated, so has its crimes. The idea of "white collar crime" dates to the early twentieth century, when the sociologist Edwin Sutherland introduced the idea in a 1939 paper he presented to the American Sociological Society called "White-Collar Criminality." [1] For Sutherland, the distinction was important, and it had everything to do with what its perpetrators looked like, who he described as "the upper or white-collar class, composed of respectable or at least respected business and professional men." He wanted to prove that sociologists and criminologists before him were wrong and that "crime is in fact not closely correlated with poverty or with the psychopathic and sociopathic conditions associated with poverty." Retroactively, he argued that "the 'robber barons' of the last half of the nineteenth century were white-collar criminals." To prove this, he pointed to the words of one of them, Cornelius Vanderbilt, who once asked the Chicago Great Western Railway executive Alpheus Beede Stickney: "You don't suppose you can run a railroad in accordance with the statutes, do you?" [2]

Vanderbilt's words perhaps best express the idea of what exactly white collar crime is. It is the world that operates outside the 'statutes,' that disregards them entirely as laws that exist for somebody else to follow, that exchanges the values of the law with the values of accumulating large amounts of money, the occupation for which Vanderbilt remains most well-known. Inherently, white collar crimes have to do with money—for this reason, Sutherland defines it as "crime in relation to businesses."

One of the most basic forms of white collar crime is corruption through bribery. It is inherently unlawful because it seeks to replace the legal process with an exchange of money. The result of bribery is that power and political favors can be bought rather than obtained through legal and democratic means. As one argument goes, the quality of goods then diminishes, in what can be called the "price" of bribery. At the same time, this makes corruption something of a scapegoat for society's collective ills. A corruption investigation is a chance for political establishments to reconfigure, as has happened in Japan in the 1980s, China in the 2000s, and Brazil in the 2010s.

Another form of white collar crime is money laundering, in which the "respectable or at least respected" face of white collar criminality does the work of converting the monetary gains of more violent forms of crime into money that can enter legal society. Like the phrase "white collar crime," the phrase "money laundering" is often attributed to a character of 1930s American life: Al Capone. As myth has it, he had been drawn to the "cash intensive business of launderettes to disguise his illegal alcohol proceeds in times of prohibition in the 1920s." [3]

Other forms of white collar crime are perhaps easier to define. Securities fraud is also known as investment fraud or sometimes Ponzi schemes. These types of fraud tend to involve either deceiving investors or manipulating the stock market. Trade secret theft is a similar crime. It involves someone stealing confidential intellectual property known as "trade secrets" for financial gain, often through fraud. In making the government's criminal case against a programmer named Anthony Levandowski—a self-driving car engineer who stole thousands of files from Google when he left Waymo and sold them to Uber—the prosecutor argues that Levandowski broke an accepted custom of not "fill[ing] our pockets on the way out the door." [4]

Arguments about justice and debates about fairness in white collar settings are the ideas that the expert viewpoints in *Opposing Viewpoints: White Collar Crime* will explore. With chapters including "Is Corruption a Major Problem?," "How Does Money Laundering Occur, and What Can Stop It?," "Can Trade Secrets Be Stolen?," and "What Makes Some Investments Illegal?," experts provide a wide range of perspectives on what white collar crime is and its impacts on the international community.

## Notes

[1] Edwin Sutherland, "White-Collar Criminality," *American Sociological Review*, February 1940. https://www.asanet.org/sites/default/files/savvy/images/asa/docs/pdf/1939%20Presidential%20Address%20(Edwin%20Sutherland).pdf

[2] Gilbert Geis, *White-Collar Criminal: The Offender in Business and the Professions*, AldineTransaction, 2007.

[3] Brigitte Unger, *Research Handbook on Money Laundering*, Edward Elgar Publishing, 2015.

[4] Charles Duhigg, "How the Anthony Levandowski Indictment Helps Big Tech Stifle Innovation in Silicon Valley," the *New Yorker*, August 28, 2019. https://www.newyorker.com/tech/annals-of-technology/how-the-anthony-levandowski-indictment-helps-big-tech-stifle-innovation-in-silicon-valley.

Chapter 1

# Is Corruption a Major Problem?

# Chapter Preface

At the root of an idea like corruption or bribery is the concept of fairness. The law is a public agreement, and inherent to that is the notion that it will apply to everyone equally. Often, however, that isn't the case. In the shadows, money changes hands in exchange for special favors and privileges. Few crimes have been part of the human condition for longer, as its fundamental logic draws from inequalities that have been part of human society from its very start. For as long as there have been laws, there have been people who have believed they are above them.

More so than most crimes, bribery is a crime where it inherently takes two to tango. There are the unscrupulous public officials who take the bribes, but there are also the wealthy individuals who use bribes in order to get what they want, whether that is evading punishment or getting around bureaucratic red tape. In that way, the dark underworld of bribes often becomes a window into needs and wants that are not being met by legal means. Often, it's in developing countries, where basic resources are not as easily accessible, where corruption is reported to run rampant and illegal shadow marketplaces reign supreme.

When most voters around the world are asked what their biggest problems with elected officials are, corruption remains an omnipresent complaint. Sometimes, like in Brazil during the 2010s, this can result in political upheaval. One of the largest anti-corruption investigations in the country's history would eventually ensnare the popular leftist politician Luiz Inácio "Lula" da Silva, preventing him from running for president in 2018 against the far-right conservative Jair Bolsonaro, who ran on promises to clean up the country's purportedly dirty political system. Just a few years later, however, Lula would end up in power again following the 2022 election.

The following chapter looks at how countries around the world look at the issue of corruption, along with who engages in it and why it matters.

VIEWPOINT 1

> *"Corrupted economies are not able to function properly because corruption prevents the natural laws of the economy from functioning freely."*

# The Negative Impacts of Corruption

*Elvin Mirzayev*

*In this viewpoint, Elvin Mirzayev lays out how political corruption on a mass scale grinds the economic gears of developing countries around the world. Instead of looking at how corruption manifests, Mirzayev examines how its impacts are distributed. He maintains that the negative effects of corruption are unevenly distributed. This stands in the way of development for countries that are most in need of it. Elvin Mirzayev is the Chief Financial Officer at a company called Norm OJSC, which is a cement producer in Azerbaijan and the South Caucasus region.*

As you read, consider the following questions:

1. How does this viewpoint say that corruption impacts prospects for innovation?
2. What are "shadow" businesses?
3. What are some of the ways that this viewpoint makes the case for corruption's trickle-down impact?

"How Corruption Affects Emerging Economies," by Elvin Mirzayev, Investopedia, December 17, 2021. Reprinted by permission.

Economies that are afflicted by a high level of corruption—which involves the misuse of power in the form of money or authority to achieve certain goals in illegal, dishonest, or unfair ways—are not capable of prospering as fully as those with a low level of corruption. Corrupted economies are not able to function properly because corruption prevents the natural laws of the economy from functioning freely. As a result, corruption in a nation's political and economic operations causes its entire society to suffer.

## Data on Corruption's Impact

According to the World Bank, the average income in countries with a high level of corruption is about a third of that of countries with a low level of corruption. Also, the infant mortality rate in such countries is about three times higher and the literacy rate is 25% lower. No country has been able to completely eliminate corruption, but studies show that the level of corruption in countries with emerging market economies is much higher than it is in developed countries.

## High Prices for Low Quality

Corruption in the way deals are made, contracts are awarded, or economic operations are carried out, leads to monopolies or oligopolies in the economy. Those business owners who can use their connections or money to bribe government officials can manipulate policies and market mechanisms to ensure they are the sole provider of goods or services in the market.

Monopolists, because they do not have to compete against alternative providers, tend to keep their prices high and are not compelled to improve the quality of goods or services they provide by market forces that would have been in operation if they had significant competition. Embedded in those high prices are also the illegal costs of the corrupt transactions that were necessary to create such a monopoly. If, for example, a home construction company had to pay bribes to officials to be granted licenses for operations, these costs incurred will, of course, be reflected in artificially high housing prices.

## Inefficiently Allocated Resources

In best practice, companies choose their suppliers via tender processes (requests for tender or requests for proposal), which serve as mechanisms to enable the selection of suppliers offering the best combination of price and quality. This ensures the efficient allocation of resources. In corrupted economies, the companies that otherwise would not be qualified to win the tenders are often awarded projects as a result of unfair or illegal tenders (e.g. tenders that involve kickbacks).

This results in excessive expenditure in the execution of projects and substandard or failed projects, leading to overall inefficiency in the use of resources. Public procurement is perhaps most vulnerable to fraud and corruption due to the large size of financial flows involved. It's estimated that in most countries, public procurement constitutes between 15% and 30% of gross domestic product (GDP).

## Uneven Distribution of Wealth

Corrupted economies are characterized by a disproportionately small middle class and significant divergence between the living standards of the upper class and lower class. Because most of the country's capital is aggregated in the hands of oligarchs or persons who back corrupted public officials, most of the created wealth also flows to these individuals.

In a corrupt economy, small businesses are not widely spread and are usually discouraged because they face unfair competition and illegal pressures by large companies that are connected with government officials. Certain industries are more prone to corruption than others, making small businesses in these sectors even more vulnerable to unethical business practices.

## Low Stimulus for Innovation

Because little confidence can be placed in the legal system of corrupted economies in which legal judgments can be rigged, potential innovators cannot be certain their invention will be protected by patents and not copied by those who know they can get away with it by bribing the authorities. There is thus a disincentive for innovation, and as a result, emerging countries are usually the importers of technology because such technology is not created within their own societies.

## A Shadow Economy Exists

Small businesses in corrupt countries tend to avoid having their businesses officially registered with tax authorities to avoid taxation. As a result, the income generated by many businesses exists outside the official economy, and thus is not subject to state taxation or included in the calculation of the country's GDP.

Another negative of shadow businesses is they usually pay their employees decreased wages, lower than the minimum amount designated by the government. Also, they do not provide acceptable working conditions, including appropriate health insurance benefits for employees.

## Low Foreign Investment and Trade

Corruption is one of the disincentives for foreign investment. Investors who seek a fair, competitive business environment will avoid investing in countries where there is a high level of corruption. While investing in emerging markets remains a popular investment area, investors are naturally hesitant to put their money at risk in countries known to have high corruption levels. Studies show a direct link between the level of corruption in a country and measurements of the competitiveness of its business environment.

## Poor Education and Healthcare

A working paper of the International Monetary Fund (IMF) shows corruption has an adverse impact on the quality of education and healthcare provided in countries with emerging economies. Corruption increases the cost of education in countries where bribery and connections play an important role in the recruitment and promotion of teachers. As a result, the quality of education decreases and this affects the overall health of the economy.

Also, corruption in the designation of healthcare providers and recruitment of personnel, as well as the procurement of medical supplies and equipment, in emerging economies results in inadequate healthcare treatment and a substandard or restricted medical supply, lowering the overall quality of healthcare.

## The Bottom Line

Many countries with emerging economies suffer from a high level of corruption that slows their overall development. The entire society is affected as a result of the inefficient allocation of resources, the presence of a shadow economy, and low-quality education and healthcare. Corruption thus makes these societies worse off and lowers the living standards of most of their populations.

VIEWPOINT

> *"When large-scale cases of corruption emerged, demonstrating that often corporate wrongdoing was not caused by rogue employees but by a specific corporate culture, the focus began to shift to aligning organizational culture with anti-corruption goals."*

# How Private Sector Corruption Works

## *The United Nations Office on Drugs and Crime*

*This excerpted viewpoint from the United Nations Office on Drugs and Crime (UNODC) provides a detailed look at how corruption impacts economies when it comes from the private sector. While cries of bribery are most often leveled at government officials or people in positions of public power, there is always someone on the other side who should probably not be offering the bribe in the first place. On the other hand, bad ethics can also come from failures in self-reporting from executives with their eyes on the bottom line. Established in 1997 under a slightly different name, the United Nations Office on Drugs and Crime focuses on studying various kinds of illegal activity around the world.*

As you read, consider the following questions:

1. In what ways were some of the early compliance programs used by regulators problematic, according to this viewpoint?
2. What is rational choice theory?
3. What does this viewpoint recommend management do to combat a corporate culture of wrongdoing?

Stricter and more nuanced regulation requires and incentivizes companies to strengthen compliance with rules, but also to focus on their values and develop an ethical culture. Stakeholders such as employees, customers, shareholders, business partners and civil society expect even higher standards of integrity and ethical business conduct than the imposition of mere rules can enforce. Focusing on rules and regulations alone will often fall short of meeting these higher expectations of ethical business practices. Therefore, an effective ethics and compliance programme, which goes beyond mere compliance and aims to foster a culture of integrity, should include internal, external and collective measures.

## From Legal to Behavioural Approaches

[…] Legal compliance approaches that merely rely on rules to be enforced by the company itself, with threats of criminal or civil punishment to back them, have historically been the primary mechanism to address corruption in the private sector. Several governments and international organizations have issued guidelines to help companies map their anti-corruption ethics and compliance programmes. UNODC, for example, has published *An Anti-Corruption Ethics and Compliance Programme for Business: A Practical Guide* and *an Anti-Corruption Ethics and Compliance Handbook for Business* (in cooperation with OECD and the World Bank). The International Standardization Organization has even approved a standardized anti-bribery management process, the ISO 37001.

However, early compliance programmes were problematic, because companies tended to focus on processes such as enacting codes of conduct and implementing internal rules and procedures without assessing the outcomes of these processes and the impact they had on ethical and behavioural issues within the companies (Hodges and Steinholtz, 2017). Therefore, such processes did not disrupt companies' problematic business models. Compliance programmes were seen as separate from core business operations, and programmes were therefore unable to change the values and working methods of the organization. As a result, corporate cultures of wrongdoing remained largely intact. When large-scale cases of corruption emerged, demonstrating that often corporate wrongdoing was not caused by rogue employees but by a specific corporate culture, the focus began to shift to aligning organizational culture with anti-corruption goals (Torsello, 2018).

Legal approaches to corporate liability addressed this shift through the lens of orthodox economics and rational choice theory (See, e.g., Becker, 1968). In a nutshell, the assumption was that the right mix of detection and sanction was the key to deterring misbehaviour. Relying exclusively on deterrence in practice is, however, too costly and ineffective, both economically and socially (Hodges and Steinholtz, 2017). Psychological and behavioural science research shows that changes in behaviour motivated by incentives and sanctions come at a high cost. These changes require the provision of financial and personnel resources, for example surveillance systems and systems of incentives and related tracking. Moreover, anti-corruption ethics and compliance programmes strongly based on detection and sanctions send a message of distrust within an organization. Surveillance can have a particularly negative impact on corporate culture. In an environment of distrust, employees may be reluctant to voluntarily observe and disclose breaches of internal policies and may feel disengaged and under continual suspicion.

To overcome a corporate culture of wrongdoing, top management needs to make clear that it does not advocate or condone wrongdoing, and that after a proper root cause analysis and investigation, intentional corruption will be punished. In technical jargon, this is often referred to as "tone from the top." Such a policy of zero-tolerance of corruption should be communicated within a framework that couples the stick of punishment with the carrot of a positive message about the type of behaviour that the company expects from its employees.

[...]

Conducting root cause analysis and investigations before determining whether punishment is required also contributes towards building a "just culture" where fairness is perceived and where people can learn from their mistakes. In such an environment, it will be possible to determine the true cause of the problem (which might be, e.g., that targets set by senior management are impossible to meet any other way) and to learn from the exercise and fix the underlying problem, rather than just blaming and punishing a scapegoat.

It is increasingly accepted that, compared to legal compliance approaches, behavioural change approaches premised on value-based programmes lead to higher levels of ethical awareness, more employees seeking advice on ethical issues, and a greater likelihood of employees reporting violations, thus minimizing damage. Value-based programmes are premised on the assumption that employees engage with whichever values are present in the company, pro-social or anti-social, and adopt them as their own. When these values are oriented towards pro-social engagement, employees are more likely to comply with rules, even when they are not monitored. Key elements in value-based programmes are treating employees fairly, rewarding ethical behaviour, remedying unintentional unethical behaviour, and punishing criminal behaviour (Treviño and others, 2006). A step further in this direction is to develop a Values Pledge. This is a collective commitment of organizations to become truly values-driven organizations and to support the creation of value-based business environments. The UK Values Alliance is a good example of an initiative which brings together individuals and companies aiming to develop a Values Pledge in the UK.

Research findings and practical experience suggest that value-based models are not only as or more effective than traditional coercion-based models, but they are also much better at encouraging voluntary compliance with the rules and lessening the difficulties and costs associated with creating and maintaining effective surveillance mechanisms needed for sanction-based models. For a broader discussion on values and value-based programmes for businesses, see Module 11 of the E4J University Module Series on Integrity and Ethics.

[...]

## Effective Anti-Corruption Ethics and Compliance Programmes

[...] Having the full support and commitment from all levels of management is essential for creating a culture that is driven by ethical values and implementing an effective anti-corruption ethics and compliance programme (UNODC, 2013b). When developing the programme, consideration needs to be given to oversight mechanisms with internal controls and record-keeping. Effective programmes also have clear, visible and accessible policies prohibiting corruption, mitigating particular corruption risks and addressing violations. They also establish channels for reporting on corruption (UNODC, 2015).

For larger companies, the programme should engage with business partners, subsidiaries and intermediaries. Employee training and the promotion and incentivizing of ethical behaviour and compliance are essential for effective implementation. The programme as a whole should be reviewed and evaluated periodically (OECD, UNODC and World Bank, 2013). The effectiveness of measures in place also needs to be improved from time to time. Larger companies are encouraged to expand measures to third parties and to share good practices, for example by participating in anti-corruption collective action projects, which are discussed further below.

Companies should not only focus on their own culture for ethics but also engage with business partners and their supply chains. Intermediaries are very often the weak link and the public perception does not only focus on the supplier itself but also on the companies that contracted them (UNODC, 2013b). In addition to ensuring compliance with national and international regulations, companies should thus adopt a proactive approach to strengthen business integrity and ethics in their supply chains, regarding their corporate responsibility and sustainable business practices.

Finally, companies can also engage in collective action such as sharing experiences in working groups or joining initiatives such as the United Nations Global Compact. In environments in which unethical practices are prevalent, companies could resort to collective action to try to change the status quo. For example, they could get regulators to intervene or set standards in areas such as supply chains. Such collective action is addressed below in further detail.

Businesses may require different approaches to create an effective ethical culture owing to their characteristics, for example, in terms of size, legal status and/or complexity. There is no one-size-fits-all model, but the underlying principles apply to both large and small companies, including start-ups (OECD, UNODC and World Bank, 2013). For example, in a large business, one manifestation of the tone from the top may be a video statement on the website or a postcard with a quote from a management representative sent to the employees, since it is not possible for the CEO to meet in person all employees. In an owner-led smaller business, one-on-one talks with the employees raising the importance of integrity as a core value of the company would be appropriate.

While a small company or start-up may not need to draft an elaborate code of ethics (although that will change as the business grows), a multinational may need to consider the best way to express its values in different contexts and pay attention to different country regulations to which its staff will be held accountable. The multinational will also need to assess the risks of unethical behaviour in the different environments in which it operates to select the appropriate controls that it needs to institute. A multinational corporation is also often faced with the problem of cultural or regional relevance. Should there be one code that applies throughout all the countries where it operates, or should there be a multiplicity of codes to make provision for different contexts? The most elegant solution is to have a global code that provides high-level guidance on the values of the company, supported by country guidelines that provide a level of flexibility, but never in contradiction with the global values or applicable law, which may be that of another jurisdiction, such as the UK Bribery Act or the US FCPA, since a multinational company may be subject to those statutes wherever it does business.

[…]

## Risk Management Approaches to Fighting Corruption in the Private Sector

[…] Corruption risk assessments are essential to ensure that resources are being applied where they most matter and to reinforce transparency, build trust and reduce corruption. To prevent and fight corruption effectively, the company needs to know how and where the crime happens. Such knowledge enables the targeting of real and not just perceived problems within a given organization's processes and structures and, eventually, the identification and application of relevant measures aimed at resolving these problems. Corruption risk assessments can be crucial because, while managers might acknowledge the risk of corruption on a more general level, they might not know or realize the exact mechanisms through which their company is exposed to corruption.

In recent years, several international organizations have developed tools and mechanisms to support the private sector's need to identify and respond to corruption risks. Such risk assessment tools have been developed, for example, by the United Nations

Global Compact, the Committee of Sponsoring Organizations of the Treadway Commission (COSO), the Regional Anti-Corruption Initiative (RAI) and Transparency International. [...]

## Business Partner's Due Diligence

To externalize business risks and for other reasons, companies sometimes outsource operations to third parties such as agents, consultants, distributors, subcontractors, re-sellers, foreign subsidiaries, business partners in joint ventures and, in general, anyone with the capacity to act on behalf of the company or whose conduct can end up benefiting the company. However, working with third parties presents significant corruption risks. For example, research from the OECD (2014) indicated that 75 percent of all transnational bribery enforcement actions conducted between 1999 and 2014 involved payments through intermediaries. The practice of using intermediaries to channel bribes is so extensive that the international community responded by tightening company responsibility by requiring due diligence to be performed when dealing with third parties.

The duty to supervise the behaviour of third parties emerges from the principle that anyone who creates a situation of risk or danger is obliged to adopt appropriate precautionary measures to serve as protection against the occurrence of the harm. To address third party risks, companies first need to map their third parties globally and understand the purpose of each commercial relationship. This information allows companies to classify their third parties into a risk matrix and adopt appropriately proportioned measures to mitigate the identified risks. In many cases, due diligence processes result in a reduction in the number of business partners and in the rationalization of operations, often to the benefit of the corporation.

Risk mitigation measures range from getting the business partners' acknowledgment and commitment to abide by the law and by the company's code of conduct to establishing contractual safeguards, including audit and termination rights, and carrying out third parties' anti-bribery training. Part of the due diligence process involves checking the reputation of potential business partners against different databases, for example those containing sanctioned persons, blacklisted persons, politically exposed persons (PEPs), and adverse media reports in local language. If the third party shows up in these lists, then the company can undertake a more thorough investigation. For a discussion of the evolution of third party due diligence, see Transparency International UK (2016).

As with employees, measures aimed at mitigating third party risks can take different shapes. Companies may concentrate on avoiding working with business partners suspected of corruption. An approach based on surveillance and sanctions will focus on the selection process of business partners and on legal measures to protect the company if the third party subsequently violates the rules. By contrast, a value-based approach aims at working with partners who share common values and at helping them to create the right corporate culture to avoid corruption. This distinction is especially important in contexts of systemic corruption, where local business partners are hired for a specific process, such as customs clearance, and obtaining licences or permits, and may have little choice but to pay bribes to deliver the goods and services to their clients. In a more coercive compliance relationship with large companies, local agents might be inclined to hide their activities. In a more open relationship, local agents can engage with large companies in a collective strategy to reduce corruption in that specific business process.

VIEWPOINT

> *"Rooting out corruption has become critical to the achievement of targets such as the United Nations' Sustainable Development Goals, while fighting this scourge is a major policy priority for development agencies and a rapidly increasing number of countries."*

# Corruption Negatively Impacts Economic and Social Development Around the World

*United Nations Office on Drugs and Crime*

*This viewpoint from the United Nations Office on Drugs and Crime outlines the ways in which corruption negatively impacts development in countries around the world. In fact, the author argues that it is the single greatest obstacle to economic and social development. This is because it weakens governments and fuels crime, which negatively impacts all areas of society. In addition to explaining the problem of corruption, this viewpoint also examines what governments, the private sector, the media, and society as a whole can do to combat it. Established in 1997 under a slightly different name, the United Nations Office on Drugs and Crime focuses on studying various kinds of illegal activity around the world.*

As you read, consider the following questions:

1. According to this viewpoint, how much money is paid in bribes around the world each year?
2. How does corruption affect the provision of services, according to this viewpoint?
3. How does corruption impact the health sector, as outlined in this viewpoint?

Corruption is the single greatest obstacle to economic and social development around the world[1]. Every year $1 trillion is paid in bribes[2] while an estimated $2.6 trillion are stolen annually through corruption—a sum equivalent to more than 35 per cent of the global GDP[3]. In developing countries, according to the United Nations Development Programme, funds lost to corruption are estimated at 10 times the amount of official development assistance (ODA)[4]. But corruption does not just steal money from where it is needed the most; it leads to weak governance, which in turn can fuel organized criminal networks and promote crimes such as human trafficking, arms and migrant smuggling, counterfeiting and the trade in endangered species.

As a result, corruption affects everyone and can lead to:

- Less prosperity: Corruption stifles economic growth, undermines the rule of law, and squanders talent and precious resources. Where corruption is rife, companies are reluctant to invest as the costs of doing business are significantly higher. In corrupt countries which are rich in natural resources, the population often does not benefit from this wealth. Corruption also weakens safety and security structures such as the police services. Ultimately, corruption prevents people, countries and businesses from fulfilling their potential.
- Less respect for rights: Corruption undermines democracy, governance and human rights by weakening State institutions that are the basis for fair and equitable societies. Vote buying at election times harms the democratic process and justice

is challenged when criminals are able to bribe their way out of trouble. Indigenous peoples and women are particularly vulnerable to corruption. Given their geographic and social exclusion, and lack of access to legal protection available to other members of society, their economic, social and cultural rights are threatened by corruption.

- Less provision of services: Corruption diverts funds intended to provide essential services such as health care, education, clean water, sanitation and housing. When officials are corrupt, this represents a major hindrance to a Government's ability to meet the basic needs of its citizens. In countries where international aid is meant to improve the quality of life, corruption denies this and can put future funding in jeopardy.
- Less employment: When jobs are given not on merit but through nepotism, opportunities are denied. Often for the poor, women and minorities, corruption means even less access to jobs. Additionally, as corruption discourages foreign investment, this leads to fewer employment opportunities.

Rooting out corruption has become critical to the achievement of targets such as the United Nations' Sustainable Development Goals, while fighting this scourge is a major policy priority for development agencies and a rapidly increasing number of countries.

As the first legally binding international anti-corruption instrument, the United Nations Convention against Corruption (UNCAC) provides a unique tool to address this global problem. In effect since December 2005, the Convention, of which UNODC is the guardian, covers four main areas: prevention; criminalization and law enforcement measures; international cooperation; and asset recovery. The Convention also contains provisions on technical assistance and information exchange and its Conference of the States Parties established a peer review mechanism in 2009. The Convention now has 177 States parties, meaning that the vast majority of UN Member States have come on board. Importantly, as the sole universal legal anti-corruption instrument, the Convention contains innovative and globally accepted anti-corruption standards applicable to both the public and private sectors.

Everyone can be a victim of corruption. Across the board, where there are corrupt practices, there is a negative impact. As these examples show, with corruption, society suffers.

## Corruption: Building Up Countries' Infrastructure or Enriching Private Bank Accounts?

When lucrative contracts are up for grabs, bribery, fraud and embezzlement can plague large-scale infrastructure projects. Corruption can lead to money being stolen and infrastructure not being built or it can result in half-built or sub-standard—and at times dangerous—infrastructure. Money can also be allocated to sectors where needs are not the greatest, but which offer the best prospects for personal enrichment. A hospital, for instance, might be sorely needed, but kickbacks for people in power could result in a far less needed project being given priority. Ultimately, as contracts are awarded to inferior companies, the quality of work is compromised. Economic ruin can result, further perpetuating underdevelopment.

Even the aftermath of disasters can provide opportunities for corrupt operators to thrive. Roads, bridges, tunnels, perhaps entire communities, have to be rebuilt. Surveyors have reported corrupt accounting and tendering practices, poor workmanship, bad planning and design, and issues with land rights in disaster-hit areas, hampering long-term recovery or reconstruction.

## Corruption: Education, Fraud and Playing with Our Children's Future

Examples of corruption in education abound. Academic fraud, for instance, is rife in many countries and is regarded as a serious threat to integrity and reliability of certification in higher education. Procurement wastage in the education sector, including school buildings, false maintenance costs and text books paid for but never received, costs the public dearly. And "ghost" or absentee teachers who feature on the list of active teachers in schools are a huge drain on public spending. As a result, educational performance among the poorest populations is severely hampered and the system's ability to deliver is harmed.

But counting the impact of corruption in education goes beyond adding up immediate financial costs. Ensuring that educational funds are invested and administered in a fair and transparent manner protects a country's most valuable asset, its children. If young people come to believe that school or university admission and marks can be bought, a country's economic and political future is in jeopardy and this entrenches a culture of corruption. Students may graduate with poor skills and thus contribute less to the economy and public sector.

## Corruption: Not Good for Your Health

Corruption results in the loss of enormous amounts of limited public health resources. For example, in developed countries, fraud and abuse in health care has been estimated to cost individual governments between $12 billion[5].

In the pharmaceutical sector, vast amounts of money—up to $50 billion—are spent every year on products: a market so large that it is extremely vulnerable to corruption.[6] Studies have shown that as much as 25 percent of medicines which are procured can be lost to fraud, bribery and other corrupt practices[7].

In certain countries, the public health system is perceived as the most corrupt public service institution—an issue which undeniably affects development. According to the World Health Organization (WHO), countries with a higher incidence of corruption have higher child mortality rates[8].

A well-functioning health sector is one of the most crucial services that a government provides to citizens. However corruption leads to national health budgets being depleted, reducing government capacity to provide essential medicines, while increasing the risk of unsafe or ineffective products on the market. It also diverts investments in necessary infrastructure such as hospitals, clinics and medical schools.

In some developing countries, pharmaceutical expenditure accounts for up to 50 percent of total health spending[9]. Given the high market value of these products they are a magnet for theft, corruption and unethical practices. Fraudulent and substandard preparations, as well as medicines that are granted unwarranted registration, cause patients needless suffering, with potentially fatal consequences.

## Corruption: Tax Bills Are Up—and You Might Not Even Be Aware

The World Economic Forum estimates that corruption increases the cost of doing business by up to 10 percent on average[10].

Corruption hinders economic development, damages private sector integrity and siphons off the finances intended to reduce poverty. Acting as a hidden "tax" or illegal overhead charge, corruption deters investors which leads to job losses and ultimately keeps a country locked in poverty. Corruption also hinders the establishment of small and medium enterprises, which can generate wealth for countries. As business trust is eroded, profits suffer, prices increase and the quality of services falls.

## Corruption: Planet Earth Being Sold Out

In spite of the significant potential of the extractive industries to generate development finance, the risk of resource leakage and corruption remains high and it needs to be tackled. Evidence suggests that the extractive sectors are associated with high levels of illicit financial flows.

Resource management is extremely important for addressing these risks. Instituting strong financial management systems with open and transparent disclosure of information on production, revenue and payments reduces the risk of embezzlement and corruption. Promoting transparency and accountability in both multinational corporations and the State is the most effective way to ensure the accountable management of revenues by the extractive sector.

The world is facing daunting environmental challenges, many exacerbated by corruption. A number of the planet's protected species are disappearing rapidly, due in part to the illegal trade in flora and fauna, and corruption comes into play as traffickers often rely on fraudulent paperwork to move parts from endangered species and illegal timber across borders.

Illegal dumping is often a result of public officials being paid off. One development consequence is that rivers may be polluted, leaving entire communities struggling to meet their daily water needs. Meanwhile corruption in the water sector puts the lives of billions of people at risk and slows development and poverty reduction efforts. Large water infrastructure projects such as dams, canals, tunnels, wells and drains, are vulnerable to bribery and procurement fraud, or contracts can be awarded to inferior firms.

## The Solutions—What Can Be Done?

Preventing and combating corruption requires a comprehensive approach, but only in a climate of transparency, accountability and participation by all members of society is this possible. Governments, the private sector, the media, civil society organizations and the general public need to work together to curb this crime. Here are some examples of how these sectors of society can make a difference.

### Governments

At the international level important conventions have been put into place to combat corruption such as the United Nations Convention against Corruption and the United Nations Convention against Transnational Organized Crime, as well as regional and sectoral instruments such as the OECD Convention on Combating Bribery of Foreign Public Officials in International Business Transactions. At the national level, governments can stimulate legislative reform that will establish legislative and institutional frameworks against corruption with robust enforcement and punitive measures.

### Private Sector

Companies should take a zero-tolerance attitude towards corruption and put policies in place covering issues such as gifts, supply chains and whistleblowers, in order to promote a fair and just environment. Through their actions and attitudes towards corruption, the business community can promote fair competition by working together and supporting countries in developing and strengthening the public anti-corruption infrastructure.

### Media

By using the often unique position that they occupy in society, the media can provide checks and balances on government and private sector involvement in corrupt practices. The media also offer an essential service in informing the public about the positive progress being made and giving support to those who take a stand in the fight against corruption.

### Citizens and Civil Society

Many civil society organizations are working hard to raise awareness, channel information from citizens to the State and exert pressure for political commitment against corruption.

As people become increasingly weary of corrupt leaders, they are demanding more accountability. Ordinary citizens, including many young people, are increasingly showing they are committed to fighting corruption in their communities and governments.

As part of this process, people can—and should—inform themselves about what their governments are doing to tackle corruption and hold elected officials responsible for their actions. Actions are also key—reporting incidences of corruption to the authorities, teaching children that corruption is unacceptable, and refusing to pay or accept bribes.

## Our Common Purpose

We all have a stake in fighting corruption.

Corruption undermines governments' ability to serve their people by corroding the rule of law, public institutions and trust in leaders. Corruption acts as a brake on development, denying millions of people around the world the prosperity, rights, services and employment which they desperately need—and deserve.

When corruption prevails, democracy, a prerequisite for development, is threatened. Sustainable development is therefore not only an aim in itself, but the most effective antidote to corruption.

With the United Nations Convention against Corruption, the world has a powerful tool to fight a global ill. Let us use the Convention's far-reaching measures to help kick-start development, lift countries out of poverty and build fairer, more just societies.

## Notes

1. International Chamber of Commerce / Transparency International / United Nations Global Compact / World Economic Forum Partnering Against Corruption Initiative. 2008. "Clean Business is Good Business." http://www.weforum.org/pdf/paci/BusinessCaseAgainstCorruption.pdf.
2. World Bank. "Six Questions on the Cost of Corruption with World Bank Institute Global Governance Director Daniel Kaufmann." http://go.worldbank.org/KQH743GKF1.

3 International Chamber of Commerce / Transparency International / United Nations Global Compact / World Economic Forum Partnering Against Corruption Initiative. 2008. "Clean Business is Good Business." http://www.weforum.org/pdf/paci/BusinessCaseAgainstCorruption.pdf.

4. UNDP. 2011. "Fighting Corruption in the Water Sector: Methods, Tools and Good Practices." http://www.undp.org/content/dam/undp/library/Democratic%20 Governance/IP/Anticorruption%20Methods%20and%20Tools%20in%20 Water%20Lo%20Res.pdf.
5. World Health Organization. 2009. "Medicines: corruption and pharmaceuticals (Fact sheet N°335)." http://www.haspi.org/curriculum-library/A-P-Core-Labs/Body%20 Chemistry/Medical%20Applications%20&%20Resources/WHO%20-%20 Corruption%20and%20Pharmaceuticals.doc.
6. WHO. "Why is good governance relevant to the pharmaceutical public sector?" http://www.who.int/medicines/areas/policy/goodgovernance/why/en/.
7. World Health Organization. 2009. "Medicines: corruption and pharmaceuticals (Fact sheet N°335)." http://www.haspi.org/curriculum-library/A-P-Core-Labs/Body%20 Chemistry/Medical%20Applications%20&%20Resources/WHO%20-%20 Corruption%20and%20Pharmaceuticals.doc.

8. World Health Organization. 2009. "Medicines: corruption and pharmaceuticals (Fact sheet N°335)." http://www.haspi.org/curriculum-library/A-P-Core-Labs/Body%20 Chemistry/Medical%20Applications%20&%20Resources/WHO%20 -%20 Corruption%20and%20Pharmaceuticals.doc.
9. World Health Organization. 2012. "Why is good governance relevant to the pharmaceutical public sector?" http://www.who.int/medicines/areas/policy/goodgovernance/why/en/.
10. World Economic Forum. International Chamber of Commerce / Transparency International / United Nations Global Compact / World Economic Forum Partnering Against Corruption Initiative. 2008. "Clean Business is Good Business." http://www.weforum.org/pdf/paci/BusinessCaseAgainstCorruption.pdf.

> *"This seems like strong evidence that the relationship between market competition and corruption depends crucially on the type of corruption."*

# The Effect of Market Competition on Corruption

*Haggai Porat*

*In this viewpoint, Haggai Porat asks whether the framework of an economic system impacts what forms corruption takes in a society. Both societies with high and low levels of market competition have their own reasons for suggesting that they can prevent some of the traditional motivations of corrupt political behavior, but there seems to be few countries that are generally thought to have succeeded at this. In fact, in both the capitalist and non-capitalist world, certain forms of corruption appear endemic. At the time this viewpoint was published, Haggai Porat was a student and researcher at Harvard Law School.*

As you read, consider the following questions:

1. According to this viewpoint, does market competition have a tendency to make societies more or less corrupt?
2. Why might competitive markets be associated with less corruption or more corruption?

"What Is the Effect of Market Competition on Corruption? Some Surprising New Findings," by Haggai Porat, GAB, November 4, 2019. Reprinted by permission.

3. What forms of bribery create competitive advantages and which kinds don't, according to Porat?

How does market competition affect the prevalence of corruption? Some people think that increasing competition could decrease corruption. The intuition is that increased competition lowers firms' profits, meaning that public officials cannot extract as much money out of the firms through extortive threats (e.g., a threat to falsely report noncompliance with safety regulations unless the firm pays a bribe). As the saying goes, you can't squeeze blood from a turnip. By contrast, the argument continues, in less competitive markets firms have higher profits, and officials, knowing this, can use threats to extract some or all of this surplus for themselves. However, others have argued that increased market competition may lead to more corruption. Those taking this position tend to emphasize collusive rather than extortive corruption and point out that increased market competition makes collusion—which is, of course, a risky proposition—more attractive to firms, because the firms have more to gain from a leg up on their competitors. For example, an importing firm that pays a bribe to avoid paying customs duty will receive greater benefit from this competitive advantage when competition is fierce, since it will allow the firm to reduce prices and increase its market share more extensively. A monopolistic importer, by contrast, has less of an interest in paying the bribe to avoid the import duty, since a monopolist can offset much of the duty by raising consumer prices without needing to worry about losing much market share.

So, one can construct plausible theoretical arguments in both directions. What does the empirical data say about which story is closer to the truth? There have been a handful of studies so far, but they provide contradictory or equivocal results—some studies find that more competitive markets are associated with less corruption, but others have found the opposite. But these studies focus on "corruption" generally, while the theories sketched above suggest that the effect of market competition on corruption may differ depending on the type of corruption—coercive or collusive. One prominent study, by Alexeev and Song (2013), explicitly incorporates this distinction and finds—based on analysis of data from the World Bank Enterprise Surveys of manufacturing firms in different countries—that increased competition increases the prevalence of collusive corruption. While this is an important step in the right direction, the survey data used here is still not ideal: the measure of "collusive corruption" is based on the respondent firms' answer to a question about the amount of money firms in their line of business typically need to pay to public officials each year "to get things done," which seems both vague and potentially overinclusive.

Luckily, later on the World Bank Enterprise Surveys expanded the range of corruption measures collected as part of its Investment Climate surveys in developing countries, recently publishing the latest of these surveys, that may shed new light on this debate. The attractive feature of this more comprehensive survey data is that, in contrast to the data used by Alxeev and Song, the new surveys ask not only about the one vague measure of corruption, but ask separately about four different kinds of informal payments: to tax officials (hereinafter tax bribe); to secure government contracts (hereinafter contract bribe); to secure an import license (hereinafter import bribe); and to secure an operating licensing (hereinafter operating bribe). The survey, both in its current and older version, further asked every firm to report the number of competitors that it faces in its market of operation, which provides a ready firm-specific measure of market competition.

A thorough analysis of the competition-corruption link using this new data will need to await future work, but as a first step, I conducted some preliminary, exploratory quantitative analysis of the Investment Climate survey data. The results were surprising, and suggest not only that asking whether "corruption" is positively or negatively correlated with market competition is too crude, but also that even the proposed collusive-coercive distinction does not adequately capture the nuances of the relationships between competition and various forms of corruption.

My preliminary analysis consisted of a multivariate statistical regression, where the primary explanatory variable of interest is the degree of market competition, and the primary outcome variables of interest are each of the four types of corruption noted above. (The regression also includes a set of control variables drawn from Alexeev & Song's prior study.) My findings were as follows:

- Higher levels of market competition have a statistically significant positive correlation with paying contract bribes and import bribes.
- Higher levels of market competition have a statistically significant negative correlation with paying tax bribes and operating bribes.

This seems like strong evidence that the relationship between market competition and corruption depends crucially on the type of corruption, but at the same time, these results do not seem consistent with the simple version of the coercion-collusion theory. It does not seem plausible that contract bribes and import bribes are clearly forms of collusive corruption, while tax bribes and operating bribes are forms of coercive corruption. Indeed, paying bribes to reduce taxes and to get operating licenses could be seen as collusive, as they advance the firm's interests. Furthermore, even if these practices include instances of coercive interaction, there is no apparent reason to think coercive tax and operating bribes would be more common than coercive contract or import bribes. So what is going on?

I would suggest that the emphasis on the coercion-collusion distinction in this context is premised on the mistaken conjecture that the relationship between market competition and corruption depends entirely on whether the firm benefits from the corrupt behavior (as in the collusive case) or is harmed by the corrupt behavior (as in the coercive case). While it is true that collusion occurs when there is a benefit to the firm from engaging in the corrupt interaction, there are different types of benefits, and only some of them are related to market competition. Specifically, we must distinguish (1) benefits that improve the firm's competitive standing, from (2) benefits that aid the firm but do not improve its competitive standing. It is only the former types of corrupt practices that we should expect to be positively correlated with market competition. Recognizing this distinction helps account for the otherwise surprising pattern I found in the Investment Climate survey data, as follows:

- Both contract and import bribes straightforwardly grant the firm that pays them a competitive advantage. Import bribes directly reduce a firm's production costs, allowing it to lower prices and secure a larger market share. Similarly, contract bribes directly increase the firm's market share by granting the firm a larger slice of the (finite) government contracting "pie." So, greater market competition means that these forms of corruption (whether we frame them as "collusive" or "coercive") are more valuable for firms, and they become more widespread. And this is consistent with my findings in the data.
- By contrast, tax bribes, even when collusive, do not necessarily create a competitive advantage. Colluding with a tax official to lower a firm's tax liability entails sharing the "profits" from this collusive deal with the public official at the expense of the state's treasury, not other firms. This sort of corruption increases a firm's profits, but it does not lower its production costs or allow the firm to do anything to lower its prices or obtain a larger market share. When the market is more competitive, firms have lower profits, and therefore there is less gain to be had from bribing tax officials. So, even when tax bribery is collusive, increased competition would be expected to result in less corruption of this type, which is consistent with what I found in the data.
- Operating bribes are harder to categorize because they might enable a firm to enter a new market. But the costs associated

> with entering a new market are sunk once the firm enters it, and therefore decreased entry costs do not give a firm any competitive advantage once it has entered that new market and is competing. Therefore, there's no reason to expect that even collusive operating bribes would be positively correlated with market competition. But what explains the negative correlation that I found in my preliminary analysis? One possibility is that the coercive nature of many of the operating bribe interactions (public officials extorting money to issue licenses to firms that meet all of the requirements) provides the explanation.

Two final notes: First, because the measure of market competition here is not a policy measure, but rather a measure of actual (and self-reported) competition, care must be taken in interpreting the results, and in deriving conclusions for policy. While the discussion here has focused on the ways in which market competition may affect the level of corruption, it's certainly possible that the causal arrow runs in the other direction as well. For example, certain markets might be less competitive in practice because the public officials in charge of granting operating licenses demand bribes, thus erecting artificial barriers to entry. Or it could be that in countries with very high tariffs, import bribes might increase market competition by allowing a larger set of firms access to important production components. Again, the analysis here is preliminary; further research, and more rigorous statistical testing, will be needed to nail down the causation question. Second, market competition is undoubtedly important for numerous reasons unrelated to corruption, and so the findings here, even if they prove robust, should not be interpreted as standalone arguments for or against attempts to foster more competitive markets. Nonetheless, it is useful for legislatures and administrative agencies tasked with promoting anticorruption policies to be more aware of the possible effects that competition may have on the prevalence of corruption, accounting for the unique economic characteristics of each corrupt practice.

Viewpoint

> *"Unfortunately, the 2021 edition of the CCC Index shows a decline in the anti-corruption environment in the majority of the countries surveyed. Brazil and Mexico were among the countries that saw their scores fall the most compared to 2020."*

# Corruption Is Still a Major Issue in Some Latin American Countries

***Geert Aalbers and Brian Winter***

*This viewpoint from Geert Aalbers and Brian Winter examines the findings of the third annual edition of the Capacity to Combat Corruption (CCC) Index, which was published in 2021. Although then-presidents Andrés Manuel López Obrador of Mexico and Jair Bolsonaro of Brazil both claimed to have tackled the issue of corruption in their respective countries, the CCC Index found that both countries had lagged in their attempts to uncover, punish, and prevent corruption. The authors argue that anti-corruption efforts have lagged throughout Latin America since the mid-2010s, and that the COVID-19 pandemic has only made this worse. Geert Aalbers is a partner and Brazil country director for Control Risks, an international risk consultancy firm. Brian Winter is editor-in-chief of* Americas Quarterly.

"One-Man Crusades Against Corruption in Latin America Aren't Working," by Geert Aalbers and Brian Winter, Americas Quarterly, June 14, 2021. Reprinted by permission.

As you read, consider the following questions:

1. What data does the CCC Index use, according to this viewpoint?
2. Which Latin American country's CCC Index score improved between 2020 and 2021?
3. How much did direct foreign investment decrease in Latin America between 2020 and 2021?

The presidents of Mexico and Brazil have very different ideologies, but they are united by at least one belief: That they have eradicated corruption in their governments.

"I can say there is no corruption. It's over because the president is not corrupt, and he doesn't tolerate the corrupt," Andrés Manuel López Obrador said at his daily press conference in March. Similarly, Jair Bolsonaro told reporters in October that he had ordered an end to Lava Jato, the country's iconic graft investigation, because "there's no more corruption in the government." He added, with a touch of irony: "When I indicate any person for any position, I know he's a good person, especially looking at the amount of criticism he receives from most of the media."

The 3rd annual edition of the Capacity to Combat Corruption (CCC) Index tells a different and more complex story. Rather than measuring perceived levels of corruption as other studies do, the CCC Index evaluates and ranks 15 Latin American countries based on their ability to uncover, punish and prevent corruption. The index, which is jointly published by Control Risks and the Americas Society/Council of the Americas (which publishes *AQ*), draws on publicly available data as well as a proprietary survey that asks in-region experts to assess a variety of factors including the independence of courts, the strength of democratic institutions and the freedom of investigative journalists. Unfortunately, the 2021 edition of the CCC Index shows a decline in the anti-corruption environment in the majority of the countries surveyed.

Brazil and Mexico were among the countries that saw their scores fall the most compared to 2020.

It's not just a tale of individual leaders or governments, of course. Anybody who lives in Latin America, or does business there, knows that anti-corruption efforts have lost momentum since the mid-2010s, when Lava Jato and similar probes sent numerous powerful politicians and business leaders across the region to jail. Since then, the perceived errors and abuses committed by a number of high-profile prosecutors and judges have contributed to a decline in popular support for investigations in some countries. As a result, politicians have seized the moment to weaken corruption-fighting institutions and safeguards. More recently, the COVID-19 pandemic led governments, citizens and civil society to shift their focus to other urgent priorities like the economy—despite numerous high-profile scandals involving the procurement of medical supplies and medicines.

But just as important as the pandemic is the widely documented erosion of democratic institutions occurring throughout much of Latin America and indeed the world in general. The CCC Index detected a concerning decline in the efficiency and independence of anti-corruption agencies in almost all the countries surveyed. The aforementioned statements from the presidents of Mexico and Brazil reflect an emerging (or "re-emerging," if one takes a longer view) belief that strong leaders are single-handedly capable of purifying their countries' politics. But we know from painful experience that this never works over time. Mexico saw its score in the CCC Index's legal capacity category decline 8% this year, and it finished ahead of only Venezuela and Bolivia in the variable assessing the independence of the chief public prosecutor. Brazil suffered similar declines, following Bolsonaro's appointment of figures perceived as less independent to the Federal Police and the Federal Public Ministry.

The news wasn't all bad. The Dominican Republic saw the biggest increase in its score, by more than a point, after President Luis Abinader appointed an attorney general widely perceived as independent. Anti-corruption enforcement also appears evenly applied—in February, Abinader fired his former health minister over the alleged purchase of overpriced medical equipment. Ecuador and Panama also saw their scores rise, following concerted efforts by governments and civil society to crack down on graft, money laundering and other ills.

But the overall trend is clear, and disconcerting. Latin America has been one of the world's regions hit hardest by the pandemic, which continues to leave a trail of death and economic destruction. Cleaner government would allow for more agile and effective responses to the numerous socioeconomic and health maladies that are likely to endure for years to come. Greater transparency would also help facilitate the boom in investment Latin America so badly needs, considering that foreign direct investment fell an estimated 50% in 2020, more than in any other region of the world.

None of these changes can be imposed from the outside—civil society, business leaders, politicians and other local actors will have to lead the process. But it's certainly possible to get the virtuous circle of healthy democracies and economies started again. Combating corruption more effectively, with strong and independent institutions front and center, building on the growing maturity of compliance in the private sector, would be a good place to start.

> *"Everyone was aware that they were illegal, and some even make fun of that in their Telegram chats."*

# A Coup of Corruption in Brazil

***Brasilwire***

*In this viewpoint on the anti-corruption investigations in Brazil, the focus turns to revelations of how those investigations were planned. This viewpoint looks at the way those allegations were weaponized by right wing political figures who were purportedly misusing the country's justice system to attack rivals with popular bases of support. In this way, it is revealed that the anti-corruption investigation was itself corrupted, though this form of anti-corruption is thought to be more political than financial in nature. BrasilWire is a website that provides independent news and analysis on Brazil in English.*

As you read, consider the following questions:

1. How did reports published by the *Intercept* in 2019 complicate the picture of Brazil's anti-corruption efforts?
2. What does this viewpoint call a "political and illegal strategy"?
3. In what ways can anti-corruption investigations be used by political parties to punish their enemies?

"New Revelations Show Sergio Moro & Lava Jato Were Central to Brazil's Coup," Brasilwire, September 8, 2019. Reprinted by permission. https://www.brasilwire.com/

Sunday 8/9/2019. An explosive report in *Folha de S. Paulo* in collaboration with *The Intercept* has revealed that Operation Lava Jato carefully edited leaks of recordings he had made, illegally, of phone calls between former President Lula and then-President Dilma Rousseff in 2016, when he was about be appointed her chief of staff.

The conversations reveal that Lava Jato Prosecutors and Sérgio Moro decided to hide excerpts of conversation which showed that Lula was reticent about accepting the position and, therefore, was not seeking to obtain immunity (*foro priviligiado*) and escape the jurisdiction of Judge Moro.

Thus, the call between Lula and former President Dilma, illegally leaked to Globo News with great fanfare, took on another context: that of a clandestine arrangement to allow Lula to avoid prosecution by "hiding" as a minister. In reality, the undisclosed conversations, some of them with the then Vice President Michel Temer, show that Lula's goal was essentially political articulation.

When the leak was made, STF minister Gilmar Mendes was pressured by TV Globo, the Military and public opinion to block Lula's appointment to Chief of Staff in a monocratic decision, thus sealing Dilma Rousseff's fate.

Her impeachment then became just a matter of time.

In a powerful and indignant text entitled "Lava Jato plotted against Lula and Dilma and changed the history of Brazil" veteran Journalist Kennedy Alencar emphasised the grave seriousness of the report:

"The report reveals that Moro, federal police and prosecutors acted to interfere with the political process in order to prevent Lula's appointment to Chief of Staff in the Dilma administration, and helped to radicalize the political environment in the country, plotting the fall of the then president, and take PT of power.

Prosecutors celebrate a political and illegal strategy. Without humanity, they call Lula "9", in a derogatory reference to the nine fingers of the President, who lost one of them in an accident at work.

## Corruption in Brazil

Operation Lava Jato started in Brazil as a money-laundering case. It quickly turned into a full-blown judicial anti-corruption crusade with far-reaching political implications across Latin America. The same companies at the heart of the Brazilian scandal offered kickbacks to public officials in at least 8 other countries. Critics see the prosecutorial zeal behind some of the national chapters of Lava Jato as yet another instance of "lawfare." For others, however, it anticipates a new era of accountability and political regeneration. In this talk we discuss our current book project, which asks two sets of questions. First, what explains why the investigation gained momentum and delivered results in some countries but not others? Our answer looks at the legacy of capacity-enhancing reforms in Latin America's prosecution services as well more immediate determinants of prosecutorial zeal. Second, we rely on focus groups and original surveys to understand the impact of Lava Jato on public opinion. What kind of emotions and attitudes towards corruption and politics do voters experience when exposed to these shocks? Does Lava Jato reinforce or curb political cynicism? Are all Lava Jatos created equal, or does the way in which different investigations unfold shape emotional and attitudinal responses?

**"The Criminalization of Corruption in Latin America: Causes and Consequences of Lava Jato," by Ezequiel González Ocantos, MIT, November 18, 2020.**

They make it clear that they were following directions from "Russo" the nickname of Moro, who acted as an inquisitor and not a judge in Lava Jato.

Everyone was aware that they were illegal, and some even make fun of that in their Telegram chats.

In this episode, they leaked what mattered to manipulate public opinion, to create street mobilizations against the government and to poison the political debate.

Moro, Federal Police agents and prosecutors kept secret Lula's conversations with then-Vice President Michel Temer in search of an understanding to avoid impeachment.

They also hid all hesitation of the petista in accepting the position of Chief of Staff.

Those who followed the real backstory and had information at the time knew that the main reason for that articulation was to try to save the government, not to obtain immunity in the Supreme Court.

But Lava Jato, aware of this, manipulated public opinion and changed the course of the country's history so that we could reach the Bolsonaro government today.

Many people have said that Lava Jato has contributed to Dilma Rousseff's impeachment.

This report shows that Lava Jato acted to have Dilma overthrown and worked illegally to arrest Lula.

This is not the role of the judicial system. It is a serious form of corruption. Public authorities are committed to the law that criminals do not have.

If the actions of Moro, Federal Police delegates and prosecutors are a legal fight against corruption, the country is fried.

It is in the hands of a parallel state that pursues political enemies. Yesterday it was Lula. Tomorrow will be the critics of these Messianics who have abused their powers.

If the Federal Supreme Court, the Attorney General's Office, the National Council of Justice, the National Council of the Public Prosecution Service, and Congress had doubts that they need to take steps to investigate and punish crimes and abuses of power by the Lava Jato stars, the *Today*'s report eliminates any hesitation or objection to a harsh response from our institutions.

Read the article. Check out Lava Jato's dialogues about Lula's conversations. Read the summaries of Lula's tapped conversations with Temer and allies.

Draw your conclusions whether they are methods of a judiciary, prosecutor and federal police of a full democracy or a banana republic.

7

VIEWPOINT

*"Brazil is experiencing the beginning of a legal scandal, which may cause the corruption investigations of recent years to collapse like a house of cards."*

# Corruption Shapes Brazil's Politics

*Transform! Europe*

*This viewpoint from Transform! Europe explains how former Brazilian president Luiz Inácio Lula da Silva—more commonly known as Lula—was prevented from running for president again in 2018 due to corruption charges brought by Sérgio Moro. The authors argue that Lula's corruption trial and his subsequent imprisonment are themselves signs of corruption, as made evident by the fact that Moro was nominated as Minister of Justice by Lula's political opponent, Jair Bolsonaro. This suggests that Moro received his nomination as compensation for bringing charges against Lula and paving the way for Bolsonaro's victory. This, in turn, suggests that corruption is deeply embedded in Brazil's political system. Transform! Europe is the political foundation of the Party of the European Left (EL) and operates across 23 countries.*

As you read, consider the following questions:

1. What political party is Luiz Inácio Lula da Silva affiliated with?
2. When was Lula imprisoned?
3. Why do the viewpoint authors argue that the charges against Lula were not legitimate?

"Judicial Conspiracy in Brazil: Prosecutors Plotted Against Lula," Transform! Europe, September 10, 2019. Reprinted by permission.

In autumn last year, rather than an investigative judge, it should have been the Brazilian people who passed their verdict on the politics of the presidential candidate for the Workers' Party (PT), Luiz Inácio Lula da Silva, during general elections.

However, the main investigative judge in the scandal regarding the government-controlled Petrobras oil corporation, Sérgio Moro, and his team of prosecutors abused their power of office to put Lula behind bars. By doing so, they prevented him from putting forward his candidacy in the October 2016 presidential elections.[1]

In 2017, after a corruption trial that lasted several years, Moro sentenced Brazil's former president (Lula was in office between 2003 and 2011) to a prison term of more than nine years. Shortly afterwards, his sentence was increased to 12 years and one month by an appellate court. 73-year-old Lula, a central figure of the Latin American left, who has been imprisoned since April 2018, had been considered a favourite for the presidential elections. However, due to his arrest, he wasn't able to stand for election. The judge's decision paved the way for Lula's opponent, the right-wing extremist politician Jair Bolsonaro, who publicly stated that he hoped Lula would "rot in prison."

Right after he took over as president, Bolsonaro nominated Moro as his Minister of Justice in the capital city of Brasília. Straight away, this appointment looked like an act of compensation for certain services. The electoral victory of the ultra right-wing politician Bolsonaro is the result of a judicial conspiracy, as revealed by *The Intercept*, an investigative platform. "Leaked mobile phone conversations"[2] between Moro and the prosecutors who were in charge of Lula's case, videos, and audio recordings prove the intentional manipulation of investigations, which were used as a political weapon against the Workers' Party (Partido dos Trabalhadores, PT). They are proof of the fact that the aim of Lula's opponents was not to carry out impartial corruption investigations, but to politically neutralise the former president.

Brazil is experiencing the beginning of a legal scandal, which may cause the corruption investigations of recent years to collapse like a house of cards. Fernando Haddad of the Workers' Party, who ran for office instead of Lula against Bolsonaro, called it "possibly the biggest scandal in the Republic's history." Since 2014, Moro, the seemingly "fearless" corruption investigator from the southern provincial city of Curitiba, has resolved one corruption case after the other in the course of Operation Car Wash ("Lava Jato"). He has been widely praised for this. The investigators from Curitiba and Judge Moro became heroes to the Brazilian right because they managed to bring Lula down.

In the case of Lula da Silva, Sérgio Moro took it as true that the former president had facilitated contracts for the OAS construction company with the partially state-controlled oil firm Petrobras. As a kickback, he is said to have received a three-floor luxury flat in the coastal town of Guarujá. However, there has never been any substantial proof of these allegations. The trial was based exclusively on mere indications. The prosecutors weren't even able to specify what kind of favour Lula had granted to the alleged "donors." There was talk of an "undefined administrative act." To this day, Lula da Silva is reaffirming his innocence and calls the proceedings against him politically motivated. "I was convicted at first instance even though no evidence was brought forward," Lula stated only recently in an interview with the German *Spiegel* magazine (22/05/2019).[3]

In early 2018, a report in the weekly newspaper *CartaCapital* caused a stir. It positioned the actions taken against Lula in the context of a continental strategy against the left in Latin America. The Dominican politician Manolo Pichardo mentioned a meeting in the American metropolis of Atlanta, during which conservative politicians from Latin America had discussed destabilising strategies along the lines of the successful "soft" coups d'état in Honduras and Paraguay, 2009 and 2012 respectively. "Our oligarchies don't lift a finger without being allowed or told to do so by the USA," Pichardo is convinced.[4]

Even the investigators themselves had massive doubts that the evidence was enough to find Lula guilty. In the decisive "leak", the chief prosecutor, Deltan Dallagnol, voiced his concerns during a chat with Judge Moro using the Telegram messenger service. He had reservations about whether the apartment was in fact Lula's and whether it had anything to do with Petrobras. Dallagnol expressed his concern about the lack of evidence, "They will say that we're pressing charges based on newspaper reports and weak evidence." This is why it was necessary to prepare for a solid public discourse.

The political beliefs of the judicial officers were revealed in another chat between the chief prosecutor Dallagnol and an unidentified contact called "Carol PGR" (Procuradoria-Geral da República, similar to the Federal Prosecutors' Office). Carol PGR: "Deltan, my friend! I'm worried about the possible return of the PT [to the government]. But I prayed a lot for God to enlighten our people and for a wonder which shall save us all." Deltan Dallagnol replied, "Thank you, Carol! Yes, pray! That's what our country needs."

The documents from 2015–2017 reveal that those involved did not just limit themselves to prayer. The then judge and incumbent Minister of Justice Moro not only colluded with the prosecutors of the Car Wash task force but gave them instructions to put Lula da Silva behind bars. He acted as an initiator and a consultant for the prosecutors, giving them advice regarding which leads to follow in their investigations. Furthermore, Moro and Dallagnol used certain tricks to make sure the case was assigned to them and not to a different court. In fact, the regional prosecutor's office in São Paulo had claimed to have taken on the case earlier.

"According to Brazilian law, this is illegal," stated Leandro Demori, the editor-in-chief of *The Intercept* Brasil. The 1988 Brazilian Constitution emphasises the independence of the judicial sector and prohibits any exchange of information between the prosecutor's office and the judge outside the trial. The judge must examine the evidence and motions presented by the prosecutors and defence attorneys, and must assess them. The judge is explicitly banned from taking part in the investigations.

The texts published by *The Intercept* demonstrate a total lack of neutrality and a direct involvement in the strategy of the prosecutor's office. Not only this, Moro had also given instructions on how to deal with the press and any potential witnesses. He pressed for searches when too much time had passed and the topic risked disappearing from the public eye. In a chat with Dallagnol he wrote, "Hasn't it already been a long time since the last investigations?" The last operation had taken place a month before and in Moro's opinion it was time to "strike" again. "That's correct," was Dallagnol's response, and three weeks later, the bell for the start of the next stage of the operation was rung.

Neither Moro nor Dallagnol have denied the content of the disclosed texts. On the contrary, after their collusion became publicly known, the incumbent Minister of Justice called talks between judges and prosecutors "normal." This is, however, absurd. "If talks between judges and investigators are common practice, they are corrupt too, since this is simply illegal," Sérgio Praça of the Brazilian think tank Fundação Getúlio said to Deutsche Welle, the German international broadcaster. Meanwhile, the federal assembly of the Brazilian Bar Association (OAB) has recommended the immediate dismissal of the Minister of Justice and the Car Wash task force. At the same time, the self-regulatory Committee of the National Council of the Public Prosecutor's Office (CNMP) has lodged a disciplinary complaint against the chief prosecutor Deltan Dallagnol.

At first, Moro's appointment as minister seemed to be a clever move by the ultra right-wing president. Now, however, the tide may turn. This is because it is no other than Bolsonaro's "super minister" who is engulfing the already battered government, consisting of right-wing conservatives, military officers and evangelicals, in crisis. For Jair Bolsonaro, the revelations of the investigative portal are coming at the worst possible moment. After a little less than six months, he is under pressure as a result of the country's economic situation. In addition, a pension reform he planned isn't making any progress. His environmental and economic policy is also highly disputed because it endangers the existence of the rainforests, amongst others.

With the support of Frente Popular and Povo Sem Medo (Nation Without Fear), the trade unions called for another general strike. The strike was against the proposed destruction of the state-regulated pension scheme, which is based on solidarity and has been working efficiently for decades, and against cuts in the education sector. In a declaration to the Brazilian People (Carta Terra, Território, Diversidade e Lutas) which was adopted by nearly 40 executive boards of trade unions and social movements, the motivations for the general strike were set out: an increase in unemployment (currently at 12.7%), wage reductions, undermining workers' rights, an increase in precarious and slave labour, cuts in social security, the minimum income policy, the liquidation of family subsidies and housing programmes, infringement of women's and youth rights, as well as budget cuts in public education.

A central demand made by the signatories was the nationwide struggle for the release of former president Luiz Inácio Lula da Silva, who was unlawfully arrested. They also asked for "respect for the constitutional and democratic rights of all people." According to the union of metalworkers, 95% of the workers participated in the strike. In large companies, such as Volkswagen, employees stopped working. According to the unions, workers went on strike in 189 cities.

## Notes

[1] Cf. Otto König/Richard Detje: Brasilien – Hexenjagd auf Ex-Präsidenten. Causa Lula kann die Linke vereinen, Sozialismus Aktuell 28/8/2018. Regarding the long-term political development in terms of the "political culture" in Latin America, see Dieter Boris: Politische Kultur in Lateinamerika. Hintergründe, Wirkungen und Perspektiven, in: Supplement der Zeitschrift Sozialismus.de 7/8-2019 (in-press).

[2] The Intercept claims to possess far more material and to have published only "a small part" of it. Apparently, there are 1,500 hours of audio and video recordings, as well as 1,700 pages of confidential documents mentioning Brazilian ministers, judges, military officers and editors-in-chief of certain media outlets. One of the founders of *The Intercept* is the journalist and Pulitzer laureate Glenn Greenwald who, in 2013, was part of the team of journalists who published the revelations made by American whistle-blower Edward Snowden regarding the NSA, the American intelligence agency.

[3] From the very beginning and despite massive criticism, the German Federal Government has been defending the proceedings against Lula. "According to the judgment of the Federal Government, there is no reason to believe the proceedings against the former Brazilian president Lula da Silva are politically motivated or contrary to the rule of law," was the government's response to a parliamentary inquiry by DIE LINKE.

[4] Gerhard Dilger: Brasiliens Ex-Präsident Lula Justizfarce gegen Lula, zweiter Akt, Neues Deutschland 25/01/2018.

## Periodical and Internet Sources Bibliography

*The following articles have been selected to supplement the diverse views presented in this chapter.*

Nate Cohn, "Threat to Democracy? Start With Corruption, Many Voters Say," *New York Times*, October 18, 2022. https://www.nytimes.com/2022/10/18/upshot/nyt-poll-threats-democracy.html.

Steve Coll, "The Trump Administration Rolls Back Anti-Corruption Efforts in the Oil Industry," *New Yorker*, August 10, 2017. https://www.newyorker.com/news/daily-comment/the-trump-administration-rolls-back-anti-corruption-efforts-in-the-oil-industry.

Adam Davidson, "Trump's Business of Corruption," the *New Yorker,* August 14, 2017. https://www.newyorker.com/magazine/2017/08/21/trumps-business-of-corruption.

Benjamin Fogel, "Against 'Anti-Corruption,'" *Jacobin*, October 5, 2018. https://jacobin.com/2018/10/corruption-bolsonaro-pt-populism-democracy-development.

Benjamin Fogel, "The Problem With 'Anti-Corruption,'" *Jacobin*, February 12, 2021. https://jacobin.com/2021/02/anti-corruption-biden-samantha-power-jake-sullivan.

Octavio García Soto, "Panama's Elites Denounce 'Corruption' — But It's Rooted in Their Economic Model," *Jacobin*, November 15, 2021. https://jacobin.com/2021/11/panamas-elites-denounce-corruption-but-its-rooted-in-their-economic-model.

Brooke Harrington, "When Reputation Matters, Leaks Like the Pandora Papers Can Be Very Effective," *New York Times*, October 8, 2021. https://www.nytimes.com/2021/10/08/opinion/pandora-papers-leak.html.

Quinta Jurecic and Benjamin Wittes, "How to Corrupt the Justice Department," the *Atlantic*, July 13, 2020. https://www.theatlantic.com/ideas/archive/2020/07/how-corrupt-justice-department/614098/.

Michael Race, "Glencore ordered to pay millions over Africa oil bribes," BBC, November 3, 2022. https://www.bbc.com/news/business-63497376.

Jonathan Rauch, "The Case for Corruption," the *Atlantic*, March 2014. https://www.theatlantic.com/magazine/archive/2014/03/the-case-for-corruption/357568/.

Michael Watson, "Corruption in the Labor Movement: From Wiseguys on the Waterfront to 'Fat, Dumb, and Happy' and Beyond," Capital Research Center, November 14, 2022. https://capitalresearch.org/article/corruption-in-the-labor-movement-part-1/.

Echo Xie, "What appointment of rising star Li Xi would mean for Xi Jinping's anti-graft drive," *South China Morning Post*, October 22, 2022. https://www.scmp.com/news/china/politics/article/3196893/guangdong-chief-li-xi-set-top-job-chinas-communist-party-anti-corruption-watchdog.

Chapter 2

# How Does Money Laundering Occur, and What Can Stop It?

## Chapter Preface

Unlike corruption, money laundering is a modern crime, implicitly tied in some way to the expansion of the global financial system. Because money is now entirely abstract—meaning it has no inherent value aside from what the market assigns to it—tracing criminal behavior is often a matter of tracing where ill-gotten funds travel and what they buy.

Consequently, criminals now generally try to "launder" that money into finances that appear to be, at least on paper, the result of perfectly legal transactions. Practically speaking, this can involve anything from using fictional "shell" businesses, to reporting earnings that are nonexistent, to buying and selling real estate in a foreign country. Doing this is a way for criminals to remove some of the primary evidence that a crime took place at all. If the money from the crime has disappeared, it becomes harder to prove it was ever there in the first place.

Money laundering makes a crime out of complicity. While a bank may not be directly involved in the violent crimes of a drug cartel, for example, bankers can be complicit by looking the other way in order to take a cut of the money those crimes generate. Consequently, most efforts by government regulators to curtail money laundering focuses on banks. Do they know where their customers' cash flows are coming from? Government regulators would like to make sure they do, but some argue that this is easier said than done.

But money isn't only laundered through banks. The luxury marketplace is especially suspectable to being used by criminals for laundering. More expensive goods can be bought in smaller quantities, quickly converting ill-gotten gains into objects that can be later resold. These kind of transactions are especially tricky to regulate because of the limited nature of the marketplace for expensive things. Only so many people can afford these things and nobody likes to lose a sale.

In this chapter, these viewpoints will both look at how the architecture of money laundering operates and some of the kinds of businesses, legal and illegal, that often get caught up in the tangled web of international crime.

> *"If investigating agencies or regulatory bodies want to check financial records, false documents are shown to confuse them."*

# How Does Money Laundering Work?

*Jagran Josh*

*In this viewpoint, the author lays out the very basics to how money laundering schemes are conducted around the world. Unlike bribery, the general idea seems to only date to the past century. In a way, this is because money laundering is something of a reactive crime, a response to the creation of an international banking and monitoring system that has made possible the close tracking of how money moves around the world. For that reason, as well, it's a crime that has quickly become increasingly popular, often directly in tune with the push of globalization. Jagran Josh is an online test preparation platform based in India.*

As you read, consider the following questions:

1. According to this viewpoint, what are the origins of money laundering?
2. What are the three main steps in laundering money?
3. How do governments try to fight money laundering?

"What Is Money Laundering and How Is It Done?" Jagran Josh. Reprinted by permission.

Money laundering refers to converting illegal earned money into legitimate money. The government does not get any tax on the money because there is no accounting of the black money. So Money Laundering is a way to hide the illegally acquired money.

## Money Laundering

The term "money laundering" is said to have originated from the mafia boss Al Capone. Capone had set up laundromats across the city as a front to disguise the original source of money which was obtained from the illegal sale of liquor during the Prohibition Era in the US.

In India, "money laundering" is popularly known as Hawala transactions.

## Meaning of Money Laundering

Money laundering refers to converting illegally earned money into legitimate money. So money laundering is a way to hide the illegally acquired money.

In the method of money laundering, money is invested in such a way that even the investigating agencies can't trace the main source of wealth. The person who manipulates this money is called "launderer."

So the black money invested into capital markets or other ventures returns back to the real money holder as the legitimate money.

## Steps Involved in Process of Money Laundering

1. Placement
2. Layering
3. Integration

### Placement

The first step in this process is the investment of black money in the market. The launderer deposits the illegal money through different agents and banks in the form of cash by having a formal or informal agreement.

### Layering

In this process, the launderer hides his real income by making foul play. The launderer deposits funds to investment instruments such as bonds, stocks, and traveler's checks or in their bank accounts abroad. This account is often opened in banks of those countries which do not reveal the details of their account holders. So in this process the ownership and source of money is disguised.

### Integration

The final stage at which the "laundered" property is re-introduced into the legitimate economy or returned back into the financial world as legal money.

## Examples of Money Laundering

There can be several ways to do money laundering, but the most popular is the establishment of the fake companies which are also known as the "shell companies." A shell company acts like a real company but in reality this company does not exist in the real world and no production takes place in such companies. Actually these shell companies exist only on paper, not in the real world.

But the launderer shows large transactions in these shell company balance sheets. He takes loans in the name of these companies, gets tax exemption from the government, does not fill income tax returns and through all these fake activities, he accumulates a lot of black money.

If investigating agencies or regulatory bodies want to check financial records, false documents are shown to confuse them.

## Other Methods of Money Laundering

Buying a large house, shop, or mall but showing less value on paper, while the actual market value of these purchased properties is much higher, is another method of money laundering. This is done so that launderers can reduce their tax burden. Thus, black money is collected through tax evasion.

In another way, money laundering takes place when the launderer deposits his black money in foreign banks. These foreign banks do not share a customer's account information with any country. For example, banks in Switzerland do not share account information where large numbers of Indians have deposited their black money.

## Prevention of Money Laundering Act, 2002 in India

The initial money laundering law in India was enacted in 2002, but it has been amended 5 times (2005, 2009 and 2012, 2015 and 2019).

The Prevention of Money-laundering Act, 2002 (PMLA) aimed at combating money laundering in India with three main objectives:

1. To prevent and control money laundering
2. To confiscate and seize the property obtained from laundered money
3. To deal with any other issue connected with money laundering in India

The PMLA (Amendment) Act, 2012 has put concealment of funds, acquisition of possessions, use of proceeds of crimes and possession of money on a criminal list.

It is worth mentioning here that RBI, SEBI and Insurance Regulatory and Development Authority (IRDA) have been brought out under the purview of PMLA, 2002. Hence the provisions of this Act shall apply to all financial institutions, banks, mutual funds, insurance companies and their financial intermediaries.

## Latest Amendments in Prevention of Money Laundering Act, 2002

The latest amendment to PMLA Act 2002 came into effect in 2019 as part of the Finance Act 2019. The primary amendment is the change in the definition of proceeds of crime under the PMLA Act, 2002.

It came into effect from 1st August 2019.

Section 3 of the PMLA Act 2002 contains provisions related to the offence of money laundering. To broaden the scope, an explanation was added to section 3 as a part of the amendment and was put into immediate effect. The explanation is as follows:

> (i) a person shall be guilty of the offence of money laundering if such person is found to have directly or indirectly attempted to indulge or knowingly assisted or knowingly is a party or is actually involved in one or more of the following processes or activities connected with proceeds of crime, namely:—
>
> (a) concealment; or
>
> (b) possession; or
>
> (c) acquisition; or
>
> (d) use; or
>
> (e) projecting as untainted property; or
>
> (f) claiming as untainted property
>
> In any manner whatsoever;
>
> (ii) the process or activity connected with proceeds of crime is a continuing activity and continues till such time a person is directly or indirectly enjoying the proceeds of crime by its concealment or possession or acquisition or use or projecting it as untainted property or claiming it as untainted property in any manner whatsoever."

On the basis of this explanation, it can be concluded that the process of money laundering is quite complex and manipulative. But the government must increase the process of digital transaction to curve the menace of corruption in the country.

Viewpoint 2

> *"These include unusual transactions out of scope with the business, nebulous origin of funds, politically-exposed persons, cash and more."*

# Banks Can Be Penalized for Not Stopping Money Laundering

*Brian Monroe*

*This viewpoint examines some of the ways that banks are expected to monitor financial transactions for potential involvement in money laundering, namely by highlighting a major Dutch bank that was punishedfor not doing that. The bank, ABN Amro, is one of the largest in the country's financial system, and the veiwpoint illuminates what kind of transactions should have been a major red flag for the bank. Brian Monroe is a writer for a blog run by the Association of Certified Financial Crime Specialists, a trade group based in Georgia.*

As you read, consider the following questions:

1. According to this viewpoint, why is individual liability considered one of the most feared arenas of compliance enforcement?

"Regional Report—Netherlands: One of country's largest banks, ABN Amro, pays nearly $600 million penalty for longstanding AML failings, lax risk ranking, missed reports on suspicious activity," by Brian Monroe, CFCS, April 28, 2021. Reprinted by permission. https://www.acfcs.org/regional-report-netherlands-one-of-countrys-largest-banks-abn-amro-pays-nearly-600-million-penalty-for-longstanding-aml-failings-lax-risk-ranking--missed-reports-on-suspicious/

2. What are some reasons that banks have trouble complying with anti-money laundering programs?
3. What is the role of banks in either combatting or facilitating money laundering?

Dutch authorities have hit the third largest bank in the Netherlands with a penalty of more than a half a billion dollars for longstanding failings in nearly every area of its fincrime compliance program, including lax customer risk scoring, shoddy alert investigations and missed reports of potential suspicious activity.

The Netherlands Public Prosecution Service (NPPS) has settled its probe into Amsterdam-based ABN Amro Bank for 480 million euros, or just less than $583 million, for falling "seriously short" of anti-money laundering (AML) compliance program requirements and being considered "culpable" in aiding criminal groups in cleansing ill-gotten gains.

The settlement, however, while lifting one specter of uncertainty for a banking group more than 300 years old, still has lingering tethers of risk in one of the most feared arenas of compliance enforcement: individual liability.

The NPPS stated that the investigation into the individuals responsible is ongoing, but the agency has already identified three former members of the bank's board of directors as being "effectively responsible" for the AML violations—a detail that should not be lost on top compliance executives, the C-suite and the typically aloof, insulated and protected board members.

Depending on the final tally of evidence gathered, these directors—and others—could be criminally prosecuted for money laundering.

In recent years, the Netherlands—along with other Nordic and Baltic regulators, investigators and watchdog bodies—has become a stronghold of compliance enforcement in Europe, levying historic, U.S.-style penalties against banks in the country, with the 2018 AML action against ING Groep approaching the $1 billion mark.

Investigators stated that between roughly 2014 and 2020—and even during a massive retooling, restructuring and staffing ramp up of AML in 2019—ABN Amro fell "seriously short" of the country's AML rules.

Those prolonged and pervasive failings—throughout foundational areas of AML, including customer due diligence and risk scoring, to the more advanced, arcane and subjective environs of alert investigations and dispositions and filing of reports on suspicious activity—gave carte blanche to "clients engaged in criminal activities . . . for a long time."

## AML Breaches at ABN Amro Both 'Serious' and 'Structural'

Investigators detailed a bevy of weaknesses and "serious shortcomings" in all areas of ABN Amro's AML program, including:

- Lack of customer diligence, data, documents: With regard to each of the four Business Lines, it was for example determined that client data or documents were missing, or that the source of data in client files was unclear.
- Tanking the risk ranking: ABN AMRO did not properly conduct client due diligence and the related risk assessment and finalized risk classification. That led to the bank assigning risk classifications to a considerable part of its clients in an incorrect manner.
- Automatons running amok: Due to a faulty automated analysis of identity data, some 5.5 million Mass Retail clients were in fact classified in the lowest risk category '00 neutral,' without adequate risk analysis, a structural failing due to a lack of due diligence depth. These gaps also bled into risk scoring tied to cash transaction expectations.
- Transaction monitoring, alert investigation, disposition: Investigators found further weaknesses tied to ABN Amro transaction monitoring, including adverse events and changes

feeding the bank into the original risk ranking—and thus re-tuning the transaction monitoring protocols more tightly to those now higher risk entities.

- Poor ratio of alerts to investigators: The transaction monitoring system structurally generated more alerts than the staff were able to handle. As a result, for several years ABN AMRO struggled with a backlog in handling alerts. There were several instances of late reporting to the country's financial intelligence unit (FIU).
- When the exit becomes a revolving door: There were shortcomings in ABN AMRO's exit process, as a result of which it could happen that the bank did not terminate relationships with clients with an 'unacceptable' risk classification, or that clients that had been exited were nonetheless able to become clients, once again.

## What Does 'Culpable Money Laundering' Mean?

Beyond broad, system-wide failings in AML prongs, programs and processes, investigators also highlighted several specific examples that constituted the foundation of the accusation of "culpable money laundering."

In short: these include unusual transactions out of scope with the business, nebulous origin of funds, politically-exposed persons, cash and more.

Overall, Dutch investigators highlighted "dozens" of instances where they believe the bank should have picked up on the aberrant activities and reported them to authorities, leading to illicit entities "abusing" accounts for their own purposes.

The failings included a panoply of suspected crimes, from tax finagling to corruption, laundering to fraud.

Here are some of the examples:

### A 'Low Risk' Tax Fracas

One client of ABN AMRO, who had been allocated the lowest risk classification, had opened a total of 192 bank accounts with ABN AMRO for 49 of their companies, between 2014 and 2018.

These accounts were mostly inactive. This client committed fiscal fraud, receiving almost EUR 200,000 from the Tax Authorities on its business accounts. Following transfer to their private accounts with ABN AMRO, most of this money was spent or withdrawn in cash by the client.

Despite the various signals and doubts that existed within ABN AMRO regarding this client, the risk classification remained low. The bank did not report unusual transactions to the FIU until the start of the criminal investigation into the client.

### Gambling with the Devil

Another client of ABN AMRO, also with a low-risk classification, was employed in the financial department of a wholesaler. The client had a gambling addiction, had debts, and his account was constantly overdrawn. ABN AMRO was aware of these problems.

The client adjusted the details of the funds of his employer's debtors, which resulted in these funds being transferred to his own bank account at ABN AMRO. Over a nine-month period, an amount in excess of EUR 4.3 million was transferred to the personal bank account of the client.

That money was then almost entirely spent gambling away.

ABN AMRO hardly performed client due diligence on this client, the client file turned out to be incomplete and the deviations from the usual transaction pattern did not generate any alerts in the transaction monitoring system.

### Negative News Corrupts Completely

Another example relates to two Dutch companies that held bank accounts with ABN AMRO. In the period 2010 through to 2017, payments passed via the accounts of these two companies totalling several tens of millions.

## Is It a Charity or a Money Laundering Scheme?

Criminals may seek to launder their money through the charity and then receive it "clean" at the other end. For example, a criminal may make a donation in cash or via online banking, either directly or through an intermediary, in order to place their money into the legitimate financial system and "layer" it to conceal its illicit source. Donations subject to unusual conditions (e.g. a particular individual or organisation being engaged to carry out work), unsolicited offers of loans to charities or a sudden request to return all or part of a donation might be intended to facilitate money laundering.

Alternatively, they may set up a beneficiary that appears legitimate, but is in fact a front for their criminal activities, in order to receive the money once it has been laundered through the charity's bank account. Tricks such as converting the money into a different currency, exchanging money for goods and back again, moving the money through multiple bank accounts across two or more jurisdictions and using an intermediary such as an NGO or a state department, are used to further obfuscate the origin of the funds.

Criminals may also seek to obtain tax or other financial benefits from making a charitable donation. For example, a criminal who pays UK tax on their legitimate activities may seek to take advantage of the fact that those who pay above the basic rate of tax can claim back the difference between the rate they pay and the basic rate on their charitable donation. Having made a charitable donation, the criminal would be able to claim that money back and it would then be ostensibly from a legitimate source.

Criminals may donate money to the charity in exchange for some other non-pecuniary benefit (e.g. a professional affiliation that will give their criminal enterprise a veneer of respectability and legitimacy).

**"The risks and penalties of money laundering for charities and how to guard against it," by Nicola Finnerty, Kinsley Napley, March 4, 2021.**

A corruption case in which these companies were supposedly involved was widely covered in national and international media since 2015. Nonetheless, it took ABN AMRO until March 2019 to first report to the FIU.

It was also found that there were shortcomings in the client due diligence regarding these two companies.

## Ratings Agencies Not Rattled on Bank After Penalty

While penalties, remediation and reputational costs for AML failings can feel costly, ratings agencies didn't pillory ABN Amro, but instead pulled out bright spots seemingly hidden among all of the bad news.

For example, even though the "identified deficiencies are serious," they "largely relate to the period before the 2019 launch of the bank's detecting financial crime comprehensive plan," according to Fitch Ratings.

As part of the mandated remediation and company-wide AML upgrades, ABN Amro strengthened its IT infrastructure, centralized AML-related controls and hired a large number of full-time employees, expected to surge to 4,200 this year, double of what it was just a year ago, at a cost of more than $500 million.

With the settlement now finalized, the sentiment from industry and outside reviewers is that Dutch authorities have assessed the bank's program, expected to be fully operational and finalized next year, to "be sufficient to restore compliance with the law."

As well, on the plus side, the investigation "did not find evidence that the bank was systematically involved in suspicious transactions or pursued high-risk customers," according to analysts.

In all, Fitch notes that the penalty will "cause a small loss in 1Q21."

But, don't fret, the seemingly hefty and statement-making settlement "will be comfortably absorbed by the bank's annual operating profit, which we expect to recover to about EUR1 billion in 2021 from close to break-even in 2020."

Only time will tell if the bank is able to execute on its promises of improvement to craft a "culture of compliance" that can, as the regulators want, put all the various pieces together.

But, at the very least, the institution is working on another aspect of compliance much ballyhooed in the United States and internationally, a "tone from the top."

"As a bank we do not merely have a legal, but also a moral duty to do our utmost to protect the financial system against abuse by criminals," ABN Amro CEO Robert Swaak said.

"In fulfilling this duty, we aim to make a meaningful contribution to a safer society," he said. "Regretfully, I have to acknowledge that in the past we have been insufficiently successful in properly fulfilling our important role as gatekeeper. This is unacceptable and we take full responsibility for this."

Viewpoint 3

> *"The whole idea of money laundering is to make it so complicated that effectively nobody could put together a chart like this."*

# Money Laundering Is Embedded in Russia's Economy

***Mark Hudspeth***

*In this viewpoint, Mark Hudspeth writes about money laundering in Russia, a country where the practice is both widespread and a large part of the country's economy. Because of the immense political power that comes with economic significance, most efforts to combat crime and money laundering in Russia comes from outside the country. By working outside the country, these efforts generally involve preventing the money from being further laundered through large purchases in other countries, often in the real estate sector. Mark Hudspeth is a producer for CBS Sunday Morning.*

As you read, consider the following questions:

1. What does this viewpoint say about the importance of money laundering to the Russian economy?
2. Was the Magnitsky Act effective in combating money laundering coming out of Russia, according to this viewpoint?

"Bill Browder on Putin, the Magnitsky Act, and Unmasking Russian Money Laundering," by Mark Hudspeth, CBS News, April 10, 2022. Reprinted by permission.

3. What's the connection between money laundering in Russia and the country's later invasion of Ukraine?

Bill Browder, an American-born, U.K.-based businessman, says the war in Ukraine is sharpening the world's focus on Russian President Vladimir Putin. "All of a sudden, the world cares about Vladimir Putin's evil," he told correspondent Seth Doane.

But that's long been clear to Browder, a Putin target himself. It was while walking in a London park that he received an alarming phone call: U.S. intelligence had learned Browder might be kidnapped and taken to Russia.

He recalled, "My safe world in London really evaporated."

Browder's decades-long odyssey with the top levels of Russian power started after he moved to Russia in the 1990s to profit from its privatization following the fall of the Soviet Union. Browder's Hermitage Fund soon became the largest foreign investment fund in the country. They researched Russian companies, initially to invest:

"What we discovered was that the oligarchs and corrupt officials who controlled these companies were stealing all the profits, all the assets, out of the companies," Browder said. "And so, the only way that I felt like I could responsibly invest is if I could figure out how they were doing the stealing and then trying to stop them."

"Not a way to make yourself very welcome in Russia?" asked Doane.

"Well, it was interesting because at the beginning of this moment, Vladimir Putin was fighting with the same guys that I was fighting with. But it turns out that he wasn't trying to end the oligarch era; he just wanted to become the biggest oligarch himself."

Browder showed Doane charts laying out the web of elaborate money-laundering operations they helped to uncover. "The money flowed from the Russian treasury through Moldova, to Latvia, then to Switzerland," said Browder. "The whole idea of money laundering is to make it so complicated that effectively nobody could put together a chart like this."

Doane asked, "It takes an investment guy who's moved to Russia to do this?"

"It takes an investment guy whose lawyer and friend was brutally murdered, and has made it his mission for the rest of his life to go after the murderers, to do this," he replied.

That lawyer and friend was Sergei Magnitsky, who'd been investigating a tax fraud scheme on Browder's behalf. "My company paid taxes to the Russian government," said Browder. "A bunch of Russian officials seized my documents, and then organized an identify theft of my companies, and then organized for a $230-million tax refund of taxes that we paid back to those stolen companies so they could enjoy the money. Sergei was the person who figured out the whole $230 million tax rebate fraud."

Magnitsky then provided testimony to the Russian state investigative committee: "But five weeks after Sergei testified, the same officials whom he testified against arrested him, put him in pre-trial detention in Russia, where he was then tortured to get him to withdraw his testimony."

Sergei Magnitsky died in a Russian jail in 2009. He was 37 years old.

"Do you feel responsible for his death?" Doane asked.

"I do."

"How do you deal with that?"

"I made a vow to his memory, to his family, to myself that I was going to devote all of my time, all of my energy, and all of my resources to go after the people who killed him, [to] make sure they faced justice," Browder replied.

He lobbied for a landmark piece of legislation called the Magnitsky Act. It originally sanctioned people linked to that tax fraud and Sergei Magnitsky's death. Signed into law in 2012, it focused attention on the sort of corruption they'd uncovered. Some of the money from that tax scheme wound up in properties purchased in London, New York and Dubai.

Browder's search for justice was the basis of a bestselling book, *Red Notice*. Now, out this week, is his latest, *Freezing Order* (published by Simon & Schuster, a division of Paramount Global, which owns CBS). It's the tale of what happened next, a true story of "money laundering, murder, and surviving Vladimir Putin's wrath."

Doane asked, "Some of this sounds like something out of a mob, mafia movie?"

"Vladimir Putin is the mafia boss," said Browder. "All of his ministers are actually, if you look at 'The Sopranos,' like the New Jersey Mafia and the Brooklyn Mafia, the Philadelphia mafia. They can all take as much money as they can steal, and they've got to pay a tribute up to the mafia boss, which is Vladimir Putin."

Browder alleges that some of that stolen $230 million ended up in the hands of Putin, a leader infamous for his shadowy wealth. The Russian president's official salary is about $140,000 annually, which raises some obvious questions about his $1.4 billion residence, his $700 million yacht, and his million-dollar watch collection.

Putin has long maintained Sergei Magnitsky died of a heart attack. His animus toward Browder was clear in his 2018 joint presidential press conference in Helsinki, when he suggested to U.S. President Donald Trump that Moscow might be willing to "swap" 12 indicted Russian military intelligence officers if the Trump administration would turn over Bill Browder to him.

"I was in shock," Browder said.

He has successfully campaigned for other countries to adopt the Magnitsky Act, to target corrupt officials and human rights abusers, and Browder is proud that now it's among the sanctions being used to punish Russia since its invasion of Ukraine.

"The story of Sergei Magnitsky is a tiny microcosm of what's now been multiplied by a million times," he said. "The people of Ukraine are bearing the criminal brunt of Vladimir Putin in the same way as we did in a very small way. And I feel heartbroken, because if people had listened more to what I was saying over the last ten years, perhaps we wouldn't be in this situation."

Viewpoint 4

> *"These absurd results are driven by government policies that force financial institutions to treat all customers as potential crooks."*

# Banks Should Not Be Responsible for Monitoring Money Laundering

***Daniel J. Mitchell***

*This viewpoint takes the position that the ways banks are forced to monitor anti–money laundering activity is too expensive and inhibits banks from lending to as many people as they would like. According to this viewpoint, the people this has the greatest potential to harm are those at the bottom of the economic system, with incomes that are less easy to trace in the international financial system. From this perspective, anti–money laundering enforcement is just another form of inept government regulation, blind to real-world conditions. Daniel Mitchell is a conservative economist who worked on former president George H. W. Bush's transition team in 1988.*

As you read, consider the following questions:

1. What are some of the additional costs of anti–money laundering regulations, according to this viewpoint?
2. How can anti-money laundering efforts hurt poor people or the economies of developing nations?

"The Government's War on Money Laundering Is Causing the Wrong Kind of Casualties," by Daniel J. Mitchell, International Liberty, January 31, 2017. Reprinted by permission.

3. What are some of the other approaches toward combatting financial crimes that this viewpoint lays out, instead of targeting money laundering?

President Trump says he wants to roll back the burden of regulation. Give the morass of red tape that is strangling the economy, this is a very worthy goal.

It's also a daunting task. Fixing the sprawling regulatory state is the modern version of cleaning the Augean stables and I'm not brimming with confidence that Trump and his appointees have Herculean powers.

That being said, if they're deciding where to focus their deregulatory efforts, cost-benefit analysis would be a very useful guide. Simply stated, go after the red tape that imposes the highest costs while yielding the fewest benefits.

And if that's the approach, so-called anti-money laundering regulations should be on the chopping block. Banks and other financial institutions are now being forced to squander billions of dollars in order to comply with laws, rules, and red tape that require them to spy on all their customers. The ostensible purpose of AML policies is to discourage criminal behavior, but experts have concluded that this approach has been a failure.

To the extent that AML policies have had an impact, it's been negative. In addition to high costs and inefficiency, the laws and regulations have disproportionately harmed poor people.

Richard Rahn, in a column for the *Washington Times*, says AML laws are the modern version of prohibition, well-meaning in theory but counter-productive in practice.

> Money laundering fits under the definition of vague law because, unlike murder or robbery, it is not a crime of an act but one of "intent." …This leads to many problems and substantial prosecutorial abuse. It is not only banks and financial institutions that are supposed to know the source of their clients' funds, but also such diverse people as car dealers, pawnbrokers, real estate agents, and on and on. Often, it is not

> considered good enough to know the source of a customer's funds (often a near-impossibility), but the source of the funds of the customer's customer. ...The result is that banks and other financial institutions increasingly refuse to open accounts for low-income people... There is a very high fixed cost for banks and others to do "due diligence" on their customers—the costs being roughly the same for a $5,000 deposit, a $500,000 deposit or a $5,000,000 deposit. Given the massive penalties banks and other financial institutions are subject to for making even an unintentional mistake, their safest course of action is to drop small customers. ...Recent academic and think tank studies show the situation only getting worse—all cost and no gain. ... the poor, including poor countries, and the honest pay a huge price for all of the additional compliance costs, which reduces productive global capital formation and real incomes.

And the price isn't trivial for the nations that get targeted, as I pointed out in testimony to the Organization for American States.

A working paper from the Center for Global Development digs into the numbers.

> The past fifteen years have seen an unprecedented level of attention on anti-money laundering...issues by financial regulators...the total value of fines levied by regulators peaked at $15 billion in 2014 in the US alone. ...Between 2010 and 2015, the Financial Action Task Force (FATF), an international group tasked with setting common AML standards across the globe, added over fifty different countries to an internationally-recognized list of high risk countries. ...there are growing concerns that this increase in regulatory activity is leading to a chilling effect on cross-border economic activity as banks limit their exposure to high risk clients or jurisdictions, a process known as 'de-risking'... This contraction of the correspondent banking network has sounded a number of alarm bells, as these services are seen as being crucial for most cross-border services... The ICC survey reported that over 40% of respondents felt that AML and know-your-customer (KYC) requirements were a significant impediment to trade finance, with nearly 70% reporting they declined transactions that year...a large

> number of money transfer companies in the US, the UK and Australia have lost access to banking services as a result of banks' desire to reduce their exposure to regulatory risk, potentially leading to a reduction to a decrease in formal remittances to developing countries, a critical source of development finance… The combined effect of all of these pressures should be leading to declines in the aggregate flow of cross-border payments.

And here are the results of the new empirical research in the study.

> The combination of large scale fines, higher compliance costs and international naming-and-shaming has—anecdotally—led many banks to withdraw from certain lines of business or geographic areas, to the potential detriment of cross-border economic activity. …We find evidence that greylisting by the FATF is consistent with up to a 10% reduction in the number of payments received by an affected country. …Issues of economic impact aside, these results suggest there is more work to be done on assessing both the effectiveness and the efficiency of the global AML/CFT regulatory regime. …First, the reduction in payments received by countries subject to greater regulatory scrutiny raises the spectre of potential losses to these countries. Second, that there is either no effect or a positive effect of FATF greylisting on the number of payments leaving a designated country suggests that increased scrutiny may not do much to prevent illicit money from leaving high risk countries and entering the international financial system at large.

In other words, lots of costs, mostly borne by poor people and poor nations, but no evidence that criminals and terrorists are being stopped.

Rather than imposing lots of red tape and requiring banks to spy on everybody, it would be much better if the government followed normal rules in the fight against crime. By all means, it should investigate real crimes, collect evidence and build cases (within proper limits), and work to punish those who inflict harm on others.

But don't squander resources in ways that aren't effective.

Some have suggested that it would make sense to have banks monitor a discrete list of potential bad guys rather than promiscuously spy on all customers.

That might be a step in the right direction, but this story from the UK-based *Times* shows that this approach leaves something to be desired.

> A controversial "blacklist" used by British banks to identify terrorists and potential money launderers has grown so bloated that it includes details of a three-year-old member of the royal family… World-Check, a database of more than two million "high-risk" individuals including criminals and senior politicians, is used by 49 of the world's 50 biggest banks to carry out compliance checks on existing and potential clients. Customers who are flagged up face extra scrutiny and their accounts…hundreds of individuals were included partly on the basis of unverified blog posts and even far-right or extremist websites.

Wow. Since some of my leftist friends consider International Liberty a "far-right" and "extremist" website, this doesn't bode well for me. I guess I'm lucky that I still have a bank account.

Here's more from the story.

> Thousands of others were listed on the database, which dates from 2014, only because they were relatives or friends of minor public figures. …Maud Windsor…was listed at nine months old. The apparent justification was that she was a family member of a "politically exposed person" (PEP), a reference to her father, who is the son of Prince Michael of Kent and 43rd in line to the throne. …Other British PEPs on the database include Sir Neil Cossons, a historian and former chairman of English Heritage. …Heather Wheeler, a Conservative MP listed on the database, told parliament this year that her bank of 30 years informed her that she was "high risk" and that it "would not deal with me anymore and that it was closing my account."

These absurd results are driven by government policies that force financial institutions to treat all customers as potential crooks.

And given the huge fines that are being levied on banks and other firms, you can understand why they drop customers and charge high fees. They are forced to act defensively.

> Thomson Reuters, the media company that makes millions of pounds compiling and selling the database, does not inform individuals if they are included and banks have no obligation to tell clients why they have been denied services. …Many financial institutions have become risk-averse… "You have an arms race where there's this immense pressure to build a 'robust' database," one expert on World-Check said. "They'll pack this database with as many names of individuals as possible. You end up getting a ton of false positives."

P.S. Statists frequently demagogue against so-called tax havens for supposedly being hotbeds of dirty money, but take a look at this map put together a few years ago by the Institute of Governance and you'll find only one supposed haven among the 28 nations listed.

P.P.S. You probably didn't realize you could make a joke involving money laundering, but here's one featuring former President Obama: https://danieljmitchell.wordpress.com/2011/09/10/barack-obamas-bank-adventure/.

P.P.P.S. But when you look at the real-world horror stories that result from these laws, you realize that the current system on money laundering is no laughing matter.

P.P.P.P.S. And you won't be surprised to learn that the statists have learned the wrong lesson. They see that AML laws have been a failure and think the right response is to go nuclear and ban cash entirely.

## Periodical and Internet Sources Bibliography

*The following articles have been selected to supplement the diverse views presented in this chapter.*

Anne Applebaum, "The Kleptocrats Next Door," the *Atlantic*, December 8, 2021. https://www.theatlantic.com/magazine/archive/2022/01/american-kleptocracy-kleptopia-united-states-dirty-money/620852.

Graham Bowley, "As Money Launderers Buy Dalís, U.S. Looks at Lifting the Veil on Art Sales," *New York Times*, June 19, 2021. https://www.nytimes.com/2021/06/19/arts/design/money-laundering-art-market.html.

Ed Caesar, "How a Young Couple Failed to Launder Billions of Dollars in Stolen Bitcoin," *New Yorker*, February 14, 2022. https://www.newyorker.com/business/currency/how-a-young-couple-failed-to-launder-billions-of-dollars-in-stolen-bitcoin.

Krystal Chia and Kiuyan Wong, "Hong Kong Arrests Two in $446 Million Money Laundering Case," *Bloomberg*, October 25, 2022. https://www.bloomberg.com/news/articles/2022-10-26/hong-kong-nabs-two-in-record-446-million-money-laundering-case.

Rebecca Heilweil, "The history of the metal box that's wrecking the supply chain," *Vox*, December 14, 2021, https://www.vox.com/recode/22832884/shipping-containers-amazon-supply-chain.

Patricia Kowsmann, "Deutsche Bank Faces Threat of Fines Over Money-Laundering Controls," *Wall Street Journal*, November 5, 2022. https://www.wsj.com/articles/deutsche-bank-faces-threat-of-fines-over-money-laundering-controls-11667644596.

Casey Michel, "The United States of Dirty Money," the *Atlantic*, October 5, 2021. https://www.theatlantic.com/ideas/archive/2021/10/how-south-dakota-became-haven-dirty-money/620298/.

Kristine Safos, "Why US Law Firms Need Anti-Money Laundering Policies," *Law360*, May 9, 2017. https://www.law360.com/articles/921886/why-us-law-firms-need-anti-money-laundering-policies.

Nicholas Shaxson, "The City of London Is Hiding the World's Stolen Money," *New York Times*, October 11, 2021. https://www.nytimes.com/2021/10/11/opinion/pandora-papers-britain-london.html.

David Smagalla, "Finra Spells Out Penalties for Anti-Money-Laundering Violations," *Wall Street Journal*, September 29, 2022. https://www.wsj.com/articles/finra-spells-out-penalties-for-anti-money-laundering-violations-11664488272.

Mengqi Sun, "DeFi Increasingly Popular Tool for Laundering Money, Study Finds," *Wall Street Journal*, January 26, 2022. https://www.wsj.com/articles/defi-increasingly-popular-tool-for-laundering-money-study-finds-11643202002.

Christian Wienberg and Frances Schwartzkopff, "Danske Shares Soar as Laundering Costs Set at $2.1 Billion," *Bloomberg*, October 27, 2022. https://www.bloomberg.com/news/articles/2022-10-27/danske-books-1-9-billion-provision-in-money-laundering-case.

Chapter 3

# Can Trade Secrets Be Stolen?

## Chapter Preface

Like banks, post offices, and the corner Dollar General, ideas can be robbed. When they are, it's called trade secret theft, a concept that dates to a number of court cases that began to show up in the mid-nineteenth century. By then, the early industrial era had begun. The economies of many of those countries were dominated by new ways of making things and new marketplaces for those things to be bought and sold.

The people behind these new ways of doing things generally believed that what they developed gave them a competitive advantage in these new marketplaces and endeavored to protect those ideas from being used by anybody else. The idea has since stuck and these so-called secrets have grown to include everything from the formula for Coca-Cola to reams of customer lists that can conveniently fit on the attachment to an email. Companies say that these are the things that make their products and business operations special, and they frequently use the legal system to protect them.

But trade secret theft is also a crime, potentially punishable with jailtime. Over the last decade, tech companies have been increasingly willing to turn over their documents to federal prosecutors in order to allow them to use the legal system to inflict punishments on disloyal former employees. And trade secret theft has increasingly become a forum for expressing geopolitical frustrations, with suspicion of "economic espionage" doled out to foreigners over anxieties about where their true loyalty lies. The U.S.'s "China Initiative," a Justice Department program that lasted from November 2018 to February 2022 and which subjected Chinese Americans and Chinese citizens legally residing in the U.S. to investigations of industrial espionage, is one such example.

The viewpoints in this chapter look at both the legal structure of how trade secrets are protected by the law as well as a number of notable instances of attempts to use those laws, and others similar to them, against alleged trade secret thieves. The chapter will also examine some of the more contentious applications of these laws, from recent moves in Silicon Valley to the Justice Department's notorious "China Initiative" project.

> *"If a person or entity discloses or publishes a trade secret while knowing it was improperly obtained, or by inducing someone to improperly obtain it, misappropriation exists."*

# What Are Trade Secrets?

***Justia***

*In the United States, one of the major laws that defines what is and is not trade secret theft is the Uniform Trade Secret Act, which was written in 1979 and has been since adopted by 48 states as well as the District of Columbia, Puerto Rico, and the U.S. Virgin Islands. Most companies believe that they conduct their business in a particular way that gives them a competitive edge over their rivals—these laws let them go to court if they believe that someone, most often a former employee, has informed their competitors about those secrets. Justia is one of the largest legal databases on the Internet.*

As you read, consider the following questions:

1. How does the Uniform Trade Secret Act define a trade secret?
2. How important is intention in defining trade secret misappropriation?
3. What happens to a trade secret once is it stolen?

Most states have adopted the Uniform Trade Secret Act (UTSA), a model law, or a modified form of it. Under the UTSA, a trade secret is defined as information that confers a competitive economic advantage over competitors that is the subject of reasonable efforts to keep it secret. If a trade secret owner does not make reasonable efforts to keep the information secret, it will no longer be a trade secret.

Trade secret infringement is called "misappropriation." It occurs when someone improperly acquires a trade secret or improperly discloses or uses a trade secret without consent or with having reason to know that knowledge of the trade secret was acquired through a mistake or accident. Misappropriation need not be intentional. It can happen inadvertently or through negligence.

Misappropriation also occurs when someone discloses or uses a trade secret without consent when, at the time of disclosure, he or she had reason to know that knowledge of the trade secret was:

- Derived from someone who obtained it through improper means;
- Obtained under circumstances that gave rise to maintain its secrecy or limit its use; or
- Derived through a person who owed a duty of confidentiality to the trade secret owner.

What counts as "improperly" acquiring a trade secret? Breaches of nondisclosure agreements, industrial espionage, theft, fraud, and bribery are all improper means of acquiring a trade secret. For example, if you hack into a company's computer and copy the files, this act of acquiring the secrets improperly is misappropriation. If you are asked to sign a nondisclosure agreement that states you can only work on secret information on company computers, and you log in to do some work on your unsecured private laptop in a public place one weekend, this may also be considered misappropriation.

If a person or entity discloses or publishes a trade secret while knowing it was improperly obtained, or by inducing someone to improperly obtain it, misappropriation exists. For example, if you run an online website and an employee of a major corporation breaches a nondisclosure agreement to give you the corporation's trade secret formula for a popular soft drink, you may be liable if you publish the formula while having facts that suggest the employee breached the nondisclosure agreement. Similarly, if you are a journalist and a source gives you encrypted files containing a secret manufacturing process, and you decrypt and publish them, you may be liable for misappropriation. A court may find that the encryption and the context in which you acquired encrypted files are reason to know that your source improperly acquired the files.

Usually, once a trade secret is misappropriated and published, it loses its status as a trade secret. Information that is known to those who could economically benefit from it no longer meets the definition for a trade secret under UTSA.

## Defenses to a Misappropriation Lawsuit

If you are accused of misappropriating trade secrets, your best defense in many states is actual independent development. Independently developing information from one's own pool of knowledge or the public domain is a complete defense to a company's claim of trade secret misappropriation. You will need to use your own files and records to prove that you completed development before any dates on which the alleged misappropriation occurred.

Related, but less strong, is a defense of reverse engineering. For example, if you reverse engineer a trade secret formula for a popular soft drink, this is not misappropriation in most states. However, you should be aware that sometimes reverse engineering is actionable under other theories. Some software comes with end-user licensing agreements in which the end user agrees to refrain from reverse engineering. Moreover, if you did not acquire the product you reverse engineered legally, that can also make this defense problematic.

Another strong defense is to attack the plaintiff's efforts to keep the information secret. A plaintiff that does not make reasonable efforts to keep information secret cannot prove a misappropriation claim. For example, it would be unreasonable to disclose trade secrets to a customer or supplier without a nondisclosure agreement. Similarly, failure to provide adequate protection to one's documents or files (such as by allowing open public access to one's offices) may be construed as a failure to use reasonable efforts at secrecy.

You can also defend on the grounds that the information that is supposedly secret is actually public. A plaintiff cannot claim as a trade secret information that is already in the public domain. With this defense, you will probably need to produce patents, articles, and books from which the trade secret information is "readily ascertainable" or revealed. However, you should be aware with this defense that unique combinations of publicly known concepts and ideas may be considered a trade secret.

Viewpoint 2

> *"Those who believe they are victims of trade secret theft by actors linked to China may, in addition to civil litigation, find a receptive audience with the DOJ."*

# How the U.S. Government Tackles Trade Secrets from China

*Todd A. Pickles*

*This viewpoint examines a U.S. Department of Justice program that began during the Trump administration called the "China Initiative," which targeted academics at U.S. universities with ties to China and sought to focus on what the agency called "economic espionage [and] theft of intellectual property." While allegations of trade secret theft are most often handled in civil courts and are punished with fines and civil damages, this campaign was notable for using the criminal justice system to go after alleged thieves of trade secrets. Todd A. Pickles is a lawyer specializing in white collar defense at the firm Greenberg Traurig LLP.*

As you read, consider the following questions:

1. What are some of the reasons the Department of Justice gave for indicating that industries in the U.S. were being hurt by the trade secret theft from China?

"DOJ's 'China Initiative' Focuses on Trade Secret Theft, Shows No Signs of Slowing Down in the Biden Administration," by Todd A. Pickles, The National Law Review, June 9, 2021. Reprinted by permission.

2. According to this viewpoint, how successful was the "China Initiative?"
3. What are some of the penalties for prosecutions stemming from the "China Initiative?"

Despite some significant policy changes at the U.S. Department of Justice (DOJ) instituted in the early months of the Biden administration, one key legal thread that remains a holdover from the prior administration appears to be the DOJ's so-called "China Initiative."

The Trump administration launched the China Initiative in late 2018 to "identify priority Chinese trade theft cases, ensure that we have enough resources dedicated to them, and make sure that we bring them to an appropriate conclusion quickly and effectively." The policy was part of an apparent trend of increased consideration by federal prosecutors and law enforcement to investigate and bring cases of trade secret theft that previously might have been viewed as best resolved through civil litigation.

According to DOJ's website, last updated in May 2021, DOJ's "China Initiative reflects the strategic priority of countering Chinese national security threats and reinforces the President's overall national security strategy." Underlying this focus, DOJ claims that "[a]bout 80 percent of all economic espionage prosecutions [by DOJ] … allege conduct that would benefit the Chinese state, and there is at least some nexus to China in around 60 percent of all trade secret theft cases."

The China Initiative is under the direction of DOJ's National Security Division (NSD), which is responsible for investigating and responding to state-actor threats to the United States. It is part of Assistant Attorney General John Demers's portfolio, who was appointed to his role leading the NSD in 2018. Demers, who previously worked at DOJ during the latter portion of the Bush administration, has remained in his position into the Biden administration. Just before the president's inauguration in January 2021, Demers credited the China Initiative with success in prosecuting cases of "economic espionage [and] theft of intellectual property." He noted that the DOJ's work through the China Initiative had bipartisan support and hoped to see a continuation of the efforts in the Biden administration. Six months into the Biden administration, that appears to be the case.

Already in 2021, DOJ has announced several new prosecutions under the China Initiative, as well as some significant convictions and sentences. For example, in February 2021, DOJ announced that a Chinese national residing in Hong Kong was indicted for conspiring to steal trade secrets from a prominent American manufacturer regarding the company's silicon carbonite technology. The case, filed in New York, was the result of an FBI investigation, including its counterintelligence unit, as well as the NSD and the United States Attorney's Office for the Northern District of New York. In announcing the charges, Assistant Attorney General Demers stated: "[t]heft of American intellectual property for the benefit of foreign firms deprives American companies of the fruits of their creativity and American workers of their jobs. The Department will do all it can to disrupt this illegal and economically destructive conduct."

More recently, in April 2021, following a 12-day jury trial, the DOJ announced the conviction of a Tennessee man for conspiracy to steal trade secrets, economic espionage, and wire fraud. The defendant had been originally charged in 2019 with trade secret theft, and new charges of economic espionage relating to the alleged involvement of Chinese governmental entities were added in 2020. DOJ had alleged that the defendant "stole valuable trade secrets related to formulations for bisphenol-A-free (BPA-free) coatings for the inside of beverage cans … to set up a new BPA-free coating company in China," and that the defendant "and her Chinese corporate partner . . . received millions of dollars in Chinese government grants to support the new company."

DOJ also announced in April 2021 that an Ohio man was sentenced to 33 months in prison for "conspiring to steal exosomerelated trade secrets concerning the research, identification, and treatment of a range of pediatric medical conditions," and his wife was sentenced to 30 months in February 2021 as part of the same scheme. DOJ alleged that the couple "started a company in China to sell the kits" based on the stolen trade secrets and that they "received benefits from the Chinese government, including the State Administration of Foreign Expert Affairs and the National Natural Science Foundation of China." In announcing these sentences, Assistant Attorney General Demers stated that "[t]his successful prosecution should serve as a warning to anyone who seeks to profit from pilfering hard-earned U.S. trade secrets."

These recent developments come on the heels of similar charges under the China Initiative, which also include criminal cases filed for visa fraud, grant fraud, export control violations, and allegations of obstruction of justice, among others. Since the creation of the China Initiative in late 2018, DOJ has brought over a dozen prosecutions of economic espionage, trade secret theft, or other federal charges. These cases are in addition to several other notable DOJ criminal prosecutions of trade secret theft that were not part of the China Initiative, and include criminal cases being filed after the commencement of civil litigation involving the same defendants.

At the same time, Congress has been active in 2021 combatting perceived efforts by some in China to illegally obtain intellectual property of U.S.-based companies or institutions. For example, on June 8, 2021, the Senate passed bi-partisan legislation called the U.S. Innovation and Competition Act of 2021, that among other things, if enacted, would require the State Department, in consultation with the DOJ, the Commerce Department, the Office of the U.S. Trade Representative, and the Director of National Intelligence, to develop a list of Chinese state-owned enterprises that have benefitted from intellectual property theft; would allow the State Department to determine aliens are inadmissible for entry by considering if their employer is involved theft of intellectual property; and would require the Treasury Department, in evaluating whether a

Chinese company listed on U.S. exchanges poses an unreasonable risk to U.S. capital markets, to consider whether the entity has "engaged in an act or a series of acts of intellectual property theft." Other bills have been proposed in the Senate and the House of Representatives with even more stringent requirements to federal agencies or penalties in response to incidents of alleged trade secret theft by individuals or entities associated with Chinese-owned companies or the Chinese government.

With the DOJ charging new defendants and achieving successes in convictions and the imposition of significant sentences under the China Initiative in 2021, there is a strong indication that the DOJ under the Biden administration will continue to investigate and criminally prosecute alleged trade secret and economic espionage by companies and individuals that are believed to have support of Chinese governmental institutions.

Consequently, those who believe they are victims of trade secret theft by actors linked to China may, in addition to civil litigation, find a receptive audience with the DOJ, both at the National Security Division at Main Justice in Washington, D.C. as well as at local United States Attorney's Offices, and may consider early notification to law enforcement such as the FBI upon discovery of possible trade secret theft. Meanwhile, individuals or companies associated with China who find themselves accused of trade secret theft may be well-served to take seriously the possibility of a criminal investigation or prosecution by the DOJ, even after the commencement of civil litigation, and to act accordingly given the substantial criminal penalties available under federal law. Regardless, it appears that the China Initiative will be a part of the DOJ's focus for the foreseeable future.

VIEWPOINT

> *"Protecting the investments and innovations of American companies is important to the FBI."*

# How Trade Secret Theft Is Prosecuted

*The Federal Bureau of Investigation*

*In this viewpoint, the Federal Bureau of Investigation (FBI) explains how they prosecuted a trade secret theft case against a former employee at General Electric (GE), who they say conspired to steal trade secrets in order to start a business that would compete with GE by selling some similar products. According to the FBI, they caught him "carrying a company laptop that had the GE trade secret files on it." After pleading guilty, he was sentenced to time served and ordered to pay his former bosses $1.4 million in restitution. The FBI is the main U.S. government agency that handles federal criminal cases.*

As you read, consider the following questions:

1. What does this viewpoint say about how agencies like the FBI police trade secret theft?
2. According to the FBI, what did former GE employee Miguel Sernas steal from the company?
3. Why is it harder to prove that Sernas and his alleged co-conspirator broke the law than it is to prove they violated GE's own policies?

"Trade Secret Theft," FBI.gov, July 29, 2020.

"He thought he was the smartest guy in the room." That's how FBI Albany Special Agent Vin Manglavil described Jean Patrice Delia, who pleaded guilty to conspiring to steal trade secrets from General Electric Company (GE). According to Manglavil, Delia was so confident that he believed he could download thousands of proprietary files—including a valuable trade secret—and launch a company to compete against his employer without anyone figuring out what he was up to.

Instead, the FBI's Albany Field Office spent the better part of seven years uncovering the duplicity of Delia and his business partner, Miguel Sernas, who was a former GE employee.

Special Agent Chris Murphy took over the case in 2017, with the support of Manglavil. The agents sifted through mounds of digital and physical evidence with the help of a team of forensic specialists, intelligence analysts, prosecutors, FBI legal attachés, and partner agencies. GE supported the investigation at every phase.

The investigation showed that Delia and Sernas stole elements of a computer program and mathematical model that GE used to expertly calibrate the turbines used in power plants.

Since GE also manufactured the turbines, they had complete understanding of them. "The company had a skill set and engineering-level details that no one else could offer," said Assistant U.S. Attorney for the Northern District of New York Wayne Myers.

Because of their expertise, power plant operators from all over the world hired GE's performance engineers to help their turbines achieve peak performance for the climate and conditions in which they were installed. The service could increase the efficiency of the turbines enough to substantially lower the plants' operating costs.

Delia worked as a GE performance engineer for eight years. He took a sabbatical in 2009 to pursue a graduate business degree in his native Canada and returned to GE in a slightly different role after completing his studies in 2011.

The investigation found that after he returned to GE, Delia began downloading thousands of files from the company's system, including ones that contained trade secrets. Delia also convinced an employee within the IT department to grant him access to files that he had no legitimate reason to see. Those files contained the proposals and cost models GE used to bid on new work and contracts. Court documents show he collected more than 8,000 files.

In May 2012, GE learned they had an unknown competitor on a bid to service a major power plant in Saudi Arabia. The competing bid came in far under what GE had quoted and at a number that was strangely similar to GE's base cost for providing the work.

When they looked into their new competitor, GE learned the company had been incorporated in Canada by Delia.

Delia resigned when he was confronted, and the FBI began its investigation soon after.

Agents Murphy and Manglavil said that it was clear from the outset that Delia and Sernas had violated company policies and acted dishonestly, but the agents and prosecutor faced a far higher hurdle in proving that the two had violated federal law by stealing a trade secret.

Over many years, the FBI obtained search warrants for the two men's email accounts and the servers and cloud storage they used for their new company. But a key break came when they arrested Sernas during a brief layover in Detroit while he was traveling from Mexico to Europe on business for the firm he started with Delia.

"Sernas was traveling on company business, carrying a company laptop that had the GE trade secret files on it," Murphy said. The investigation also uncovered evidence that Sernas and Delia had sent the calculations over email and uploaded them to cloud storage accounts.

Sernas pleaded guilty to conspiring to steal trade secrets and was sentenced in December 2019 to time served and ordered to pay restitution of $1.4 million to GE. Delia also pleaded guilty to conspiracy to steal trade secrets and is scheduled to be sentenced next month. He faces up to 87 months in prison under the federal sentencing guidelines.

Murphy said protecting the investments and innovations of American companies is important to the FBI: "This case shows that the FBI continues to work every day, even if it takes several years, to hold criminals accountable for their actions."

Viewpoint 4

> *"Much of the history of innovation is, in fact, also a history of theft."*

# The Effect of Trade Secrets on Big Tech

*Charles Duhigg*

*This viewpoint casts a critical eye toward how enforcement of trade secret laws has impacted corporate culture in Silicon Valley, home to some of the largest tech companies in the U.S. Charles Duhigg looks at the example of a notorious engineer named Anthony Levandowski, who had been hired to develop a self-driving car for Google and then was accused of taking some of that technology to Uber. Duhigg, however, makes the case that this is a major part of how much of the tech industry had developed in the first place. Duhigg is a tech reporter who won a Pulitzer Prize in 2013 for a series of stories the* New York Times *published on the business practices of Apple. At the time this viewpoint was published, he wrote for the* New Yorker.

As you read, consider the following questions:

1. How much were the documents that Anthony Levandowski allegedly stole worth?
2. How did the Economic Espionage Act, passed in 1996, make it easier for the federal government to pursue anyone accused of stealing corporate secrets?

3. What does this writer say is one of the problems with how that law is both written and enforced?

When a federal prosecutor announced on Tuesday morning that Anthony Levandowski, who was once hailed as the savant of self-driving cars, was being charged with thirty-three criminal acts of trade-secret thievery, he framed it as a victory for law and order. "All of us have the right to change jobs," U.S. Attorney David Anderson told reporters in San Jose, California. But Levandowski, the prosecutor said, had engaged in more than just job-hopping when he left his employer, Google, to make his way to a competitor, Uber, in 2016. Rather, Levandowski had stolen Google's intellectual property. "None of us has the right to fill our pockets on the way out the door," Anderson said. "Theft is not innovation."

Much of the history of innovation is, in fact, also a history of theft: Microsoft stole the basic idea for the graphical user interface (think Windows' on-screen icons) from Apple; Apple had stolen it from Xerox; the researchers at Xerox, most likely, stole it from someone else. Innovation, in many ways, is not about creation but about iteration, about building on ideas that have come before. Innovation is also about betrayal: much of Silicon Valley's genesis can be traced to Fairchild Semiconductor, which was founded by a group of young engineers who came to be known as the Traitorous Eight after they left their previous employer, en masse, to set up a rival company. The reason the technology industry has flourished in Silicon Valley, many economists argue, is that California makes it so easy to betray, cheat, and steal. The state's founding commercial laws generally prohibit companies from constraining their employees with "non-compete clauses." As a result, for most of the state's history, workers could jump from company to company, carrying secrets in their heads, as often as they liked, cross-pollinating as they flitted across the digital landscape.

The difference today is that now there are just a handful of large tech companies—and some of those giants, after benefitting from theft, are worried that they might be on the wrong side of the purloiner dynamic going forward. And so many of them are now issuing to workers a basic threat: if you leave and join a competitor, we might come after you for stealing our secrets. And the titans, apparently, have found a willing enforcer in the federal government.

As I wrote last year, Levandowski, who is thirty-nine years old, is one of the founding figures in the ongoing race to build autonomous cars. His insights were valuable enough that Google, at one point, promised to give him more than a hundred million dollars if he helped the search company build a self-driving vehicle. Eventually, Levandowski left Google and made his way to Uber, which was trying to build autonomous cars of its own. In the weeks before his departure, Levandowski downloaded about fourteen thousand files, including some Google hardware schematics. He transferred those files to an external drive and then wiped his laptop clean. The actual value of the files has been hotly debated—one Google engineer dismissed them as "low value" information—but there was sufficient pretense for Google to file a $1.85 billion lawsuit against Uber, in 2017, arguing that Levandowski had stolen trade secrets. When the case went to trial, the following year, it captivated Silicon Valley. Until, that is, everything fizzled: Google essentially threw in the towel after four days in court, settling for a small bit of Uber stock valued, at the time, at about two hundred and fifty million dollars (which, to a Valley mogul, hardly justifies getting out of bed). Perhaps more valuable to the company, the settlement established an "independent software expert" who can review Uber's autonomous-driving technology to insure that none of Google's proprietary information is used or replicated. Levandowski, by then, had been fired by Uber, and throughout the lawsuit he remained mum, asserting his Fifth Amendment right against self-incrimination when asked virtually any question.

And so, it seemed, that was it—until Tuesday, when the U.S. Attorney revealed that Levandowski had been indicted by a grand jury on thirty-three counts of "theft and attempted theft of trade

## How Financial Crime Supports Violent Crime

Any crime which results in a profit can be used to finance terrorism. This means that a country may face terrorism finance risks even if the risk of a terrorist attack is low.

Sources of terrorist funding include, but are not limited to, low-level fraud, kidnapping for ransom, the misuse of non-profit organizations, the illicit trade in commodities (such as oil, charcoal, diamonds, gold and the narcotic "captagon"), and digital currencies.

By disrupting the flow of terrorist funding and by understanding the funding of previous attacks, we can help prevent attacks in the future.

The example below shows how our global network of countries, alerts and specialized support can lead to fast and concrete results in investigations.

One of our member countries in Europe requested assistance with a live terrorist financing investigation in which the suspect had financed the travel of family members and others to conflict zones by transferring funds valued circa EUR 18,000.

Our specialized officers offered advice in order to streamline the investigation and liaised with four other member countries from Africa, Americas and the Middle East where funds had been transferred.

At the request of the investigating country, INTERPOL published a Red Notice for the suspect who was subsequently arrested in another, previously unconnected, member country and extradited for prosecution.

**"Tracing Terrorist Finances," Interpol.**

secrets," and that, "if convicted, the defendant faces a maximum sentence of 10 years and a fine of $250,000, plus restitution, for each violation." During Silicon Valley's genesis, federal prosecutors were unable to charge a U.S. citizen for such a crime. But, in 1996, Congress, in an attempt to combat the foreign theft of American intellectual property, passed the Economic Espionage Act, which made it easier for the federal government to pursue anyone who stole corporate secrets. The law was mostly intended to be used against overseas saboteurs, but it has largely been directed at American citizens—and, in effect, has made federal prosecutors into heavies operating on behalf of disgruntled tech firms. A federal official who worked on trade-secret investigations told me last year that Silicon Valley companies "couldn't be more two-faced about" coöperating with prosecutors. "They want good P.R.," and so they publicly disdain intrusive government investigations, the official said. "But privately they're, like, 'Hey, we'll take the subpoena, and we'll even help you write it.' "

The indictment against Levandowski is scarce on details. It does, however, declare that "in or about 2007, 2009, and 2012, levandowski signed employment agreements with Google. Each employment agreement contained, among other provisions, a Confidential Information paragraph, which obligated levandowski to hold Google's Confidential Information, including trade secrets, in confidence." If the government proves successful in its prosecution, it will likely be because of this work-around to California's prohibition on non-compete clauses. Levandowski, prosecutors are claiming, was free to leave Google—as long as he didn't carry any secrets he had learned with him.

The problem, though, is that the definition of a "trade secret" in the statute is so broad that it could very well mean anything. Daniel Olmos, an attorney who has represented individuals accused of stealing trade secrets, told me last year that "I get calls all the time from scared engineers, who once put some work stuff on their home computer so they could work on it after dinner, and now they're worried if they try to jump to another firm they're gonna get sued. And you know what? They're right to be worried." Olmos said that if a company looks closely enough at anyone's digital history they will likely find something they can use to accuse him of stealing trade secrets—a thumb drive inserted into a computer, say, or a file e-mailed to oneself. As a result, employees remain in their current jobs. "The easiest decision is usually to ignore the recruiter's call," Olmos said.

Tuesday's indictment is drawing mixed reviews in Silicon Valley. Some were delighted by the possibility that Levandowski could be sent to prison. He had clearly taken files from Google that he was not supposed to take—and he is widely disliked (and, at one time, was envied) by his former colleagues. "He's one of the most coin-operated people I've ever met," a former co-worker told me. "He just goes wherever they pay him the most." Others have been put off by his extracurricular activities, such as his founding of a church, called the Way of the Future, devoted to "the realization, acceptance, and worship of a Godhead based on Artificial Intelligence." "I guess while Anthony Levandowski is cooling in the pokey, he can pray to his AI god," one tech writer tweeted on Tuesday. Greed and blind techno-utopianism, of course, are hardly uncommon in the technology industry. But Levandowski is, in many ways, a perfect mirror of the Valley's worst instincts, and so, like many perfect mirrors, folks are happy to see him get broken if it means they no longer have to suffer the glare.

But some people are also troubled by the arrest, because of what it portends for worker mobility in the technology industry. Silicon Valley benefits from allowing workers to move from firm to firm, spreading ideas in a manner that might disadvantage their old, spurned employers but that, on the whole, accelerates innovation over all. If Levandowski is convicted, the precedent may have a chilling effect. "This situation makes me wonder how any person specializing in cutting edge technology would ever consider jumping from one development project to another competing project," one observer wrote on Reddit. "You instantly become a target: Something experimental that Company X was working on shows up in Company Y's final project? Who are they immediately going to point the finger at?"

The Valley is, in general, a fearful place right now, and Tuesday's indictment will only increase those anxieties. As Levandowski pleaded not guilty to all charges, his court appearance was live-tweeted. ("No tie," one observer wrote. "Bold move.") His father, stepmother, and a friend pledged their homes as guarantees for

Levandowski's two-million-dollar bond. Afterward, Levandowski exited the courthouse through a phalanx of cameras recording his every movement. But the Google executives who spurred this investigation and willingly handed over databases and documents to help prosecutors get the evidence they needed received no such scrutiny. They remained anonymous and in the background, lucky beneficiaries of all the thefts and secrets that had come before. Now the odds of those secrets moving among firms quite so easily has changed. As Anderson, the U.S. Attorney, said on Tuesday morning, everyone still has the right to change jobs. Now, though, we should all be a bit more worried about what we're carrying in our heads—and our pockets—as we walk out the door.

# Periodical and Internet Sources Bibliography

*The following articles have been selected to supplement the diverse views presented in this chapter.*


Katie Benner, Paul Mozur, and Raymond Zhong, "Huawei Said to Be Under U.S. Investigation in Trade-Secrets Case," *New York Times*, January 16, 2019. https://www.nytimes.com/2019/01/16/technology/huawei-investigation-trade-secrets.html.

James Bessen, "How Companies Kill Their Employees' Job Searches," the *Atlantic*, October 17, 2014. https://www.theatlantic.com/business/archive/2014/10/how-companies-kill-their-employees-job-searches/381437/.

Keith Bradsher, "How China Obtains American Trade Secrets," *New York Times*, January 15, 2020. https://www.nytimes.com/2020/01/15/business/china-technology-transfer.html.

Robert Burnson, "China-Bound Ex-Apple Engineer Admits to Trade Secrets Theft," *Bloomberg*, August 22, 2022. https://www.bloomberg.com/news/articles/2022-08-22/ex-apple-engineer-pleads-guilty-in-trade-secrets-theft-case.

Charles Duhigg, "Did Uber Steal Google's Intellectual Property?" *New Yorker*, October 15, 2019. https://www.newyorker.com/magazine/2018/10/22/did-uber-steal-googles-intellectual-property.

Peter J. Henning, "What Is a Trade Secret? A Key Question in the Case Against Anthony Levandowski," *New York Times*, September 10, 2019. https://www.nytimes.com/2019/09/10/business/dealbook/levandowski-trade-secret-uber.html.

Aarian Marshall, "Waymo v. Uber's Big Question: What on Earth Is a Trade Secret, Anyway?" *Wired*, February 6, 2018. https://www.wired.com/story/waymo-uber-trial-kalanick-testimony/.

Francis Morrison, "When A Claimed Trade Secret Isn't in Fact A Secret," *Law360*, June 7, 2022. https://www.law360.com/articles/1498396/when-a-claimed-trade-secret-isn-t-in-fact-a-secret.

Jack Queen, "'Overheated': How A Chinese-Spy Hunt at DOJ Went Too Far," *Law360*, September 28, 2021. https://www.law360.com/articles/1425776.

Matt Reynolds, "Upside Foods Sues an Ex-Employee Over Secret Lab-Grown Meat Tech," *Wired*, December 13, 2021. https://www.wired.com/story/upside-foods-blue-sky-trade-secrets-lawsuit/.

David Uberti, "Court Ruling Reflects Latest Pressure on AI Trade Secrets," *Wall Street Journal*, February 4, 2021. https://www.wsj.com/articles/court-ruling-reflects-latest-pressure-on-ai-trade-secrets-11612485559.

Aruna Viswanatha, Kate O'Keeffe, and Dustin Volz, "U.S. Accuses Chinese Firm, Partner of Stealing Trade Secrets from Micron," *Wall Street Journal*, November 1, 2018. https://www.wsj.com/articles/u-s-accuses-two-firms-of-stealing-trade-secrets-from-micron-technology-1541093537.

Debby Wu and Cagan Koc, "ASML Warns Chinese Rival May Be Infringing Its Trade Secrets," *Bloomberg*, February 9, 2022. https://www.bloomberg.com/news/articles/2022-02-09/asml-warns-chinese-rival-may-be-infringing-its-trade-secrets?leadSource=uverify%20wall.

# Chapter 4

# What Makes Some Investments Illegal?

## Chapter Preface

An investment is never certain. It runs the risk of losing value but tantalizes with the promise of growing in value instead. Some investments, however, are considered by the law to be illegal, which is where the viewpoints in this chapter converge.

The Ponzi scheme is considered the classic form of this kind of theft, in which investors discover they are not putting their money into a business, but instead are paying older investors to make it seem like they are making a profit and encourage more investors to join. When the scheme is outed, the business is revealed to have been a mirage. Charles Ponzi, for instance, had told investors that the dip in currency exchange rates in Europe after World War I meant that postage coupons could be bought cheaply there and then resold in the U.S. for more money. Bernie Madoff told investors that he had invented an idea called "split strike conversion," which involved buying and selling stocks from the S&P 100 at "opportunistic times" that would evade downswings in market. In reality, these proved to be fictional sales that never happened. Instead, Madoff used the money clients "invested" to pay clients who wanted to cash out their investments. The nature of investment scams is ever-changing and has grown to include cryptocurrencies, which are often used to buy non-fungible tokens (NFTs). Since NTFs and cryptocurrencies have no inherent value, they can be easily manipulated for scams.

Insider trading is a trickier form of investment crime. The inside trader is deliberately buying and selling stocks in advance of their increase or decrease in value based on information that will impact their price but hasn't been made public yet. Because it is dependent on having access to information about the inner workings of a company or industry, its perpetrators can often include prominent and powerful figures, like businesswoman and media personality Martha Stewart or Chris Collins, a former congressman from New York.

The viewpoints in this chapter investigate the ways that these investment-related crimes take place and the ways they are policed. They also consider the larger corporate and legal culture that forms around these investment scams and crimes.

Viewpoint 1

> "Madoff's apparently ultra-high returns persuaded clients to look the other way."

# The Infamous Case of Bernie Madoff

*Adams Hayes*

*This viewpoint tells the story of one of the most infamous financial scammers of the twenty-first century so far, Bernie Madoff. By various accounts, Madoff was able to swindle approximately $65 billion from the various people and investment funds that had trusted him with their investments. He won over these clients with the promise of high returns, which he was often able to deliver. After running out of money during the financial crisis in 2008, when too many clients decided to withdraw money at once, he turned himself in. Adams Hayes is a financial writer at Investopedia with a background in derivatives trading.*

As you read, consider the following questions:

1. What was Bernie Madoff's background before getting into the investment world?
2. What economic event precipitated the collapse of Madoff's financial scam?
3. According to this viewpoint, how did Madoff's investment scam work?

Bernard Lawrence "Bernie" Madoff was an American financier who executed the largest Ponzi scheme in history, defrauding thousands of investors out of tens of billions of dollars over the course of at least 17 years, possibly longer.

He was also a pioneer in electronic trading and chair of the Nasdaq in the early 1990s. He died in prison at age 82 on April 14, 2021, while serving a 150-year sentence for money laundering, securities fraud, and several other felonies.

## Early Life and Education

Bernie Madoff was born in Brooklyn, New York, on April 29, 1938, to Ralph and Sylvia Madoff. His father worked as a plumber before entering the financial industry with his wife. They founded Gibraltar Securities, which was ultimately forced to close by the SEC.

Bernie earned a bachelor's degree in political science from Hofstra University in 1960 and briefly attended law school at Brooklyn Law School. While in college, Bernie married his high-school sweetheart, Ruth (née Alpern), with whom he later founded Bernard L. Madoff Investment Securities LLC in 1960.

At first, he traded penny stocks with $5,000 he earned installing sprinklers and working as a lifeguard. He soon persuaded family friends and others to invest with him. When the "Kennedy Slide" flash crash lopped 20% off the market in 1962, Madoff's bets soured and his father-in-law had to bail him out.

## Notable Accomplishments

Madoff had a chip on his shoulder and felt that he was not part of the Wall Street in-crowd. In an interview with journalist Steve Fishman, Madoff advised, "We were a small firm, we weren't a member of the New York Stock Exchange. It was very obvious."

According to Madoff, he began to make a name for himself as a scrappy market maker. "I was perfectly happy to take the crumbs," he told Fishman, giving the example of a client who wanted to sell eight bonds; a bigger firm would disdain that kind of order, but Madoff's would complete it.

Success finally came when he and his brother Peter began to build electronic trading capabilities—"artificial intelligence" in Madoff's words—that attracted massive order flow and boosted the business by providing insights into market activity. "I had all these major banks coming down, entertaining me," Madoff told Fishman. "It was a head trip."

He and four other Wall Street mainstays processed half of the New York Stock Exchange's order flow—controversially, he paid for much of it—and by the late 1980s, Madoff was making in the vicinity of $100 million a year.

Madoff would become chair of the Nasdaq in 1990, and also served in 1991 and 1993.

## Scandal, Scheme, and Crime

At some point, Madoff attracted investors by claiming to generate large, steady returns through an investing strategy called split-strike conversion, a legitimate trading strategy. However, Madoff deposited client funds into a single bank account that he used to pay existing clients who wanted to cash out.

He funded redemptions by attracting new investors and their capital but was unable to maintain the fraud when the market turned sharply lower in late 2008.

On Dec. 10, 2008, he confessed his wrongdoing to his sons—who worked at his firm. The following day, they turned him over to the authorities. Bernie remained adamant that his sons were not aware of his scheme.

The fund's last statements indicated it had $64.8 billion in client assets.

## The Players

It is not certain when Madoff's Ponzi scheme began. He testified in court that it started in the early 1990s, but his account manager, Frank DiPascali, who had been working at the firm since 1975, said the fraud had been occurring "for as long as I remember."

Even less clear is why Madoff carried out the scheme at all. "I had more than enough money to support any of my lifestyle and my family's lifestyle. I didn't need to do this for that," he told Fishman, adding, "I don't know why." The legitimate wings of the business were extremely lucrative, and Madoff could have earned the Wall Street elites' respect solely as a market maker and electronic trading pioneer.

Madoff repeatedly suggested to Fishman that he was not entirely to blame for the fraud. "I just allowed myself to be talked into something and that's my fault," he said, without making it clear who talked him into it. "I thought I could extricate myself after a period of time. I thought it would be a very short period of time, but I just couldn't."

The so-called Big Four—Carl Shapiro, Jeffry Picower, Stanley Chais, and Norm Levy—have attracted attention for their long and profitable involvement with Bernard L. Madoff Investment Securities LLC. Madoff's relationships with these men go back to the 1960s and 1970s, and his scheme netted them hundreds of millions of dollars each.

"Everybody was greedy, everybody wanted to go on and I just went along with it," Madoff told Fishman. He indicated that the Big Four and others (several feeder funds pumped client funds to him, some all but outsourcing their management of clients' assets) must have suspected the returns he produced or at least should have. "How can you be making 15 or 18% when everyone is making less money?" Madoff said.

## The Scheme

Madoff's apparently ultra-high returns persuaded clients to look the other way. In fact, he simply deposited their funds in an account at Chase Manhattan Bank—which merged to become JPMorgan Chase & Co. in 2000—and let them sit. The bank, according to one estimate, may have made as much as $435 million in after-tax profit from those deposits.

When clients wished to redeem their investments, Madoff funded the payouts with new capital, which he attracted through a reputation for unbelievable returns and grooming his victims by earning their trust. Madoff also cultivated an image of exclusivity, often initially turning clients away. This model allowed roughly half of Madoff's investors to cash out at a profit. These investors have been required to pay into a victims' fund to compensate defrauded investors who lost money.

Madoff created a front of respectability and generosity, wooing investors through his charitable work. He also defrauded a number of nonprofits, and some had their funds nearly wiped out, including the Elie Wiesel Foundation for Peace and the global women's charity Hadassah. He used his friendship with J. Ezra Merkin, an officer at Manhattan's Fifth Avenue Synagogue, to approach congregants. By various accounts, Madoff swindled $2.4 billion from its members.

Madoff's plausibility to investors was based on several factors:

- His principal, public portfolio appeared to stick to safe investments in blue-chip stocks.
- He claimed to be using a collar strategy, also known as a split-strike conversion. A collar is a way of minimizing risk, whereby the underlying shares are protected by the purchase of an out-of-the-money put option.
- His returns were high (10 to 20% per annum), consistent, and not outlandish. As the *Wall Street Journal* reported in a now-famous interview with Madoff, from 1992:

> [Madoff] insists the returns were really nothing special, given that the Standard & Poor's 500-stock index generated an average annual return of 16.3% between November 1982 and November 1992. "I would be surprised if anybody thought that matching the S&P over 10 years was anything outstanding," he says.

## The Investigation

The SEC had been investigating Madoff and his securities firm off and on since 1992—a fact that frustrated many after he was finally prosecuted since it was felt that the biggest damage could have been prevented if the initial investigations had been rigorous enough.

Financial analyst Harry Markopolos was one of the earliest whistleblowers. In 1999, he calculated in the space of an afternoon that Madoff had to be lying. He filed his first SEC complaint against Madoff in May 2000, but the regulator ignored him.

In a scathing 2005 letter to the Securities and Exchange Commission (SEC), Markopolos wrote, "Madoff Securities is the world's largest Ponzi Scheme. In this case, there is no SEC reward payment due to the whistle-blower so basically I'm turning this case in because it's the right thing to do."

Many felt that Madoff's worst damage could have been prevented if the SEC had been more rigorous in its initial investigations.

Using what he called "Mosaic Theory," Markopolos noted several irregularities. Madoff's firm claimed to be making money even when the S&P was falling, which made no mathematical sense, based on what Madoff claimed he was investing in. The biggest red flag of all, in Markopolos's words, was that Madoff Securities was earning "undisclosed commissions" instead of the standard hedge fund fee (1% of the total plus 20% of the profits).

The bottom line, concluded by Markopolos, was that "the investors that pony up the money don't know that BM [Bernie Madoff] is managing their money." Markopolos also learned Madoff was applying for huge loans from European banks (seemingly unnecessary if Madoff's returns were as high as he said).

It was not until 2005—shortly after Madoff nearly went belly-up due to a wave of redemptions—that the regulator asked Madoff for documentation on his trading accounts. He made up a six-page list, the SEC drafted letters to two of the firms listed but didn't send them, and that was that. "The lie was simply too large to fit into the agency's limited imagination," writes Diana Henriques, author of the book *The Wizard of Lies: Bernie Madoff and the Death of Trust* which documents the episode.

The SEC was excoriated in 2008 following the revelation of Madoff's fraud and their slow response to act on it.

## The Punishment

In November 2008, Bernard L. Madoff Investment Securities LLC reported year-to-date returns of 5.6% during the same period when the S&P 500 dropped 39%. As the selling continued, Madoff became unable to keep up with a cascade of client redemption requests.

So, on Dec. 10, according to the account he gave Fishman, Madoff confessed to his sons Mark and Andy, who worked at their father's firm. "The afternoon I told them all, they immediately left, they went to a lawyer, the lawyer said, 'You gotta turn your father in,' they went, did that, and then I never saw them again." Bernie Madoff was arrested on Dec. 11, 2008.

Madoff insisted he acted alone, though several of his colleagues were sent to prison. His elder son Mark Madoff died by suicide exactly two years after his father's fraud was exposed. Several of Madoff's investors also died by suicide. Andy Madoff died of cancer at age 48 in 2014.

Madoff was sentenced to 150 years in prison and forced to forfeit $170 billion in 2009. His three homes and four boats were auctioned off by the U.S. Marshals. On Feb. 5, 2020, Madoff's lawyers requested that Madoff be released early from prison claiming that he was suffering from a terminal kidney disease that may kill him within 18 months.

However, Madoff, prisoner No. 61727-054, remained at the Butner Federal Correctional Institution in North Carolina until he died on April 14, 2021.

## The Aftermath

The paper trail of victims' claims displays the complexity and sheer size of Madoff's betrayal of investors. According to documents, Madoff's scam ran for more than five decades, beginning in the 1960s. His final account statements, which include millions of pages of fake trades and shady accounting, show that the firm had $47 billion in "profit."

While Madoff pleaded guilty in 2009 and was sentenced to spend the rest of his life in prison, thousands of investors lost their life savings, and multiple tales detail the harrowing sense of loss victims endured.

Investors victimized by Madoff have been helped by Irving Picard, a New York lawyer overseeing the liquidation of Madoff's firm in bankruptcy court. Picard has sued those who profited from the Ponzi scheme; by April 2021, he had recovered nearly $14 billion.

In addition, a Madoff Victim Fund (MVF) was created in 2013 to help compensate those Madoff defrauded, but the Department of Justice didn't start paying out any of the roughly $4 billion in the fund until late 2017. Richard Breeden, a former SEC chair who is overseeing the fund, noted that thousands of the claims were from "indirect investors"—meaning people who put money into funds that Madoff had invested in during his scheme.

Since they were not direct victims, Breeden and his team had to sift through thousands and thousands of claims, only to reject many of them. Breeden said he based most of his decisions on one simple rule: Did the person in question put more money into Madoff's funds than they took out? Breeden estimated that the number of "feeder" investors was north of 11,000 individuals.

In a September 2021 update for the Madoff Victim Fund, Breeden wrote, "MVF is thrilled to announce a new distribution totaling $568,648,065 to 30,539 victims of the crimes committed at Madoff Securities. Measured by the number of victims paid, this is our largest distribution yet." With the completion of the seventh distribution of funds in September 2021, approximately $3.762 billion has been distributed to 39,494 Madoff victims in the U.S. and around the world. Breeden also noted that they have recovered 81.35% for victims.

## Who Started the Ponzi Scheme?

Charles Ponzi was a man whose name went down in history for the "scheme" he developed to take money from unsuspecting investors. Since the days of Charles Ponzi, his money-grabbing scam has been replicated by countless white collar criminals on scales from large to small.

Charles Ponzi's name became associated with the word "Ponzi Scheme" in the 1920s after authorities and investors discovered the Ponzi had defrauded millions of dollars from his trusting investors. The Ponzi scheme worked by taking money from new investors to pay older investors. The scam involved the purchase of discounted postage coupons with investor money. What was really happening was, as new investors joined the pool and sent money, Ponzi would use this money to pay the older investors. The scam was earning Ponzi himself over $250,000 a day.

Ponzi primarily targeted working-class people who dreamed of becoming wealthy through investing. Ponzi was later sentenced to serve 14 years in prison. It's said that he later moved to Brazil, where he died a poor man.

Ponzi became so famous for his legendary scam that his name was tied to the deceptive criminal method he used. To this day, everyone knows the term Ponzi to be a type of investment fraud.

Not all individuals who are accused of running a Ponzi scheme are actually guilty of the offense. If you've been accused of a criminal act like this, you might want to look into the legal options you can employ for your defense. You might have powerful criminal defense strategies at your disposal that can assist you in defending against your charges.

**"What's the history of the 'Ponzi scheme?'," The Goldberg Law Firm, December 14, 2018.**

## Depictions of Bernie Madoff in Popular Culture

As a financial antagonist, Bernie Madoff has been depicted as a villain in the media and pop culture. For instance, in a 2009 episode of HBO's *Curb Your Enthusiasm*, Jason Alexander (who played George on *Seinfeld*) is swindled by Madoff and loses all of his money made off of a fictional app that he invented. Other fictional characters have also been had by Madoff (or similar knock-offs) such as a couple in Woody Allen's film *Blue Jasmine*, and the protagonist of Elinor Lipman's novel, *The View from Penthouse B*.

Madoff himself has also been depicted in several incarnations, from a 2010 theatrical production called *Investing with Madoff* to an ABC miniseries starting Richard Dreyfuss. In 2017, Madoff was played by Robert DeNiro in the HBO film *The Wizard of Lies*. Several documentaries, books, and journalistic accounts have also featured Bernie Madoff in describing his fraud and subsequent demise.

## Who Was Bernie Madoff?

Bernie Madoff was an American financier and former Nasdaq chair who orchestrated the largest Ponzi scheme in history. Bernie promised investors high returns in exchange for their investments. However, rather than investing, he deposited their money into a bank account and paid, upon request, from existing and new investors' funds. During the 2008 recession, he could no longer accommodate redemption requests. His scheme came to an end after his sons turned him over to authorities. Bernie was convicted of fraud, money laundering, and other related crimes, for which he was sentenced to 150 years in federal prison. Bernie Madoff died in prison on April 14, 2021, at the age of 82.

## How Much Money Did Bernie Madoff Return?

In addition to being sentenced to prison, Bernie Madoff was ordered to pay back $170 billion of investors' money. Madoff's assets, including real estate, yachts, and jewelry, were seized and sold by the Feds. Separately, The Bernie Madoff Victims Fund, led by Richard Breeden, has recovered and paid more than $3.7 billion to close to 40,000 victims as of September 2021.

## How Did Madoff Get Caught?

Although several people alerted the SEC and other authorities of Bernie Madoff's scheme, it wasn't until he confessed to his sons that he was caught. In 2008, when Bernie could no longer accommodate investors' redemption requests, he admitted his wrongdoings to his sons, Mark and Andrew, who then turned their father over to authorities.

## The Bottom Line

In 2009, at age 71, Madoff pleaded guilty to 11 federal felony counts, including securities fraud, wire fraud, mail fraud, perjury, and money laundering. The Ponzi scheme became a potent symbol of the culture of greed and dishonesty that, to critics, pervaded Wall Street in the run-up to the financial crisis. Madoff, the subject of numerous articles, books, movies, and biopic miniseries, was sentenced to 150 years in prison and ordered to forfeit $170 billion in assets, but no other prominent Wall Street figures faced legal ramifications in the wake of the crisis. In April 2021, Madoff died in a federal correctional facility at age 82.

Viewpoint 2

> *"Regardless of the stance individuals take, insider trading is currently illegal and can be severely punished through fines and time in prison."*

## What Is Insider Trading?

*Andrew Sabastian*

*Another type of crime in the world of financial investment is insider trading, which deals with utilizing non-public information in order to determine the best time to buy and sell investments. In this viewpoint, Andrew Sabastian looks at some of the arguments for why insider trading doesn't harm as many people as the law presumes it does—after all, most non-public information becomes public at some point. Perhaps because of the ease of committing insider trading, it remains one of the more common forms of white collar crime. Sebastian is a writer at Investopedia with a background in advising on investing strategies.*

As you read, consider the following questions:

1. How is insider trading defined in this viewpoint?
2. What are some of the arguments in support of insider trading provided in this viewpoint?
3. What's an example of an insider trading scheme?

"Arguments for and Against Insider Trading," by Andrew Sabastian, Investopedia, January 30, 2022. Reprinted by permission.

A debate rages on in the financial community among professionals and academics about whether insider trading is good or bad for markets. Insider trading refers to the purchase or sale of securities by someone with information that is material and not in the public realm.

Insider trading is not limited to company management, directors, and employees. Outside investors, brokers, and fund managers can also violate insider trading laws if they gain access to nonpublic information.

## Arguments for Insider Trading

One argument in favor of insider trading is that it allows nonpublic information to be reflected in a security's price and not just public information. Critics of insider trading claim that would make the markets more efficient.

As insiders and others with nonpublic information buy or sell the shares of a company, for example, the direction in price conveys information to other investors. Current investors can buy or sell on the price movements, and prospective investors can do the same. Prospective investors could buy at better prices, while current ones could sell at better prices.

### Delaying the Inevitable?

Another argument in favor of insider trading is that barring the practice only delays the inevitable and leads to investor errors. A security's price will rise or fall based on material information.

Suppose an insider has good news about a company but cannot buy its stock. Then those who sell in the time between when the insider knows the information and when it becomes public are prevented from seeing a price increase. Barring investors from readily receiving information or getting that information indirectly through price movements can lead to errors. They might buy or sell a stock that they otherwise would not have traded if the information had been available earlier.

Laws against insider trading, especially when vigorously enforced, can result in innocent people going to prison. As rules become more complex, it becomes harder to know what is or is not legal resulting in participants accidentally breaking the law without knowing so.

For example, someone with access to material nonpublic information might accidentally disclose it to a visiting relative while talking over the phone. If the relative acts on that information and gets caught, the person who accidentally disclosed it might also go to prison. These sorts of risks increase fear to the point where talented people pursue careers elsewhere.

Warning: If you happen to get material nonpublic information, do not make any investment decisions based on it until that information becomes public. Also, never share material nonpublic information with outsiders.

Yet another argument for allowing insider trading is that it is not serious enough to be worth prosecuting. The government must spend its limited resources on catching nonviolent traders to enforce laws against insider trading. There is an opportunity cost to going after insider trading because the government must divert those resources from cases of outright theft, violent assaults, and even murder.

## Arguments Against Insider Trading

One argument against insider trading is that if a select few people trade on material nonpublic information, then the public might perceive markets as unfair. That could undermine confidence in the financial system and retail investors will not want to participate in rigged markets.

Insiders with nonpublic information would be able to avoid losses and benefit from gains. That effectively eliminates the inherent risk that investors without the undisclosed information take on by investing. As the public gives up on markets, firms would have more difficulty raising funds. Eventually, there might be few outsiders left. At that point, insider trading could eliminate itself.

### Investors Without Nonpublic Information

Another argument against insider trading is that it robs the investors without nonpublic information of receiving the full value for their securities. If nonpublic information became widely known before insider trading occurred, the markets would integrate that information, resulting in accurately priced securities.

Suppose a pharmaceutical company has success in Phase 3 trials for a new vaccine and will make that information public in a week. Then, there is an opportunity for an investor with that nonpublic information to exploit it.

Such an investor could purchase the pharmaceutical company's stock before the public release of the information. The investor could significantly benefit from a rise in the price after the news is made public by buying call options. The investor who sold the options without knowledge of the success of the Phase 3 trials probably would not have done so with full information.

## The Legality of Insider Trading

Certain types of insider trading have become illegal through court interpretations of other laws, such as the Securities Exchange Act of 1934. Insider trading by a company's directors can be legal as long as they disclose their buying or selling activity to the Securities and Exchange Commission (SEC) and that information subsequently becomes public.

For many years, insider trading laws did not apply to members of Congress. Some lawmakers sought to profit from material nonpublic information during the 2008 financial crisis, bringing this issue to the public's attention. Congress overwhelmingly passed the STOCK Act to remedy this situation, and President Barack Obama signed it into law in 2012.

## Example of Insider Trading

An example of insider trading involves Michael Milken, known as the Junk Bond King throughout the 1980s. Milken was famous for trading junk bonds and helped develop the market for below-investment-grade debt during his tenure at the now-defunct investment bank Drexel Burnham Lambert.

Milken was accused of using nonpublic information related to junk bond deals that were being orchestrated by investors and companies to take over other companies. He was charged with using such information to purchase stock in the takeover targets and benefiting from the rise in their stock prices on the takeover announcements.

Suppose the investors selling their stock to Milken had known that bond deals were being arranged to finance the purchase of those companies. There's a good chance they would have held onto their shares to gain from the appreciation. Instead, the information was nonpublic and only people in Milken's position could benefit. Milken eventually pleaded guilty to securities fraud, paid a $600 million fine, was banned from the securities industry for life, and served two years in prison.

## The Bottom Line

Insider trading has both proponents and critics. Those against insider trading believe that it tips the balance in favor of those with nonpublic information. Advocates of insider trading believe that it avoids risks and makes markets more efficient.

Regardless of the stance individuals take, insider trading is currently illegal and can be severely punished through fines and time in prison.

VIEWPOINT 3

> "What could be more immoral than someone's selling or buying stock on the basis of information he knows the other party lacks?"

# Not All Trading by Insiders Is Insider Trading

*Financial Spread Betting*

*In this viewpoint, a writer for the blog Financial Spread Betting considers some common criticisms of the idea of insider trading. All inside knowledge eventually becomes widely known, and it's nearly impossible to have the full picture anyway, this argument goes. As a somewhat popular example of insider trading, he brings up the conviction of the lifestyle TV icon Martha Stewart, who went to jail for five months in a case that involved alleged insider trading regarding shares of a company called ImClone. The blog Financial Spread Betting is focused on discussing stock trading information and strategies.*

As you read, consider the following questions:

1. According to this viewpoint, why is the line between prohibited inside knowledge and permissible inside knowledge far from clear?
2. Who are the victims of insider trading schemes?
3. From a legal perspective, what did Martha Stewart do wrong?

"The Effects of Stock Market Insider Trading," Financial Spread Betting. Reprinted by permission. https://www.financial-spread-betting.com/Effects-of-stock-market-insider-trading.html

It is virtually unquestioned in America today that stock market insider trading in the securities markets is a dastardly act. We must make a distinction here between trading by insiders and trading by insiders on the basis of nonpublic information. Insiders are legally allowed to buy and sell stocks. The Securities and Exchange Commission (SEC) requires insiders to disclose their trades, and the financial newspapers report such trading. Investors find this information a source of valuable clues about companies. (It is possible that even without the SEC requirement, shareholders would require their executives and directors to declare their trades.)

But what could be more immoral than someone's selling or buying stock on the basis of information he knows the other party lacks?

Put that way, maybe it doesn't seem so immoral after all. The idea that knowledge can ever be evenly distributed is one of those utopian pipe dreams the realization of which would require nothing less than secret police and gulags. Knowledge, like everything else about people, is most definitely unevenly "distributed." It is not distributed at all. It is acquired—by effort or luck. It's not as though there is a central knowledge-giver who spitefully shortchanges some of us. This leads to the first observation: if the law prohibits people from exploiting knowledge advantages, they have less incentive to ferret out valuable knowledge and bring it to market. Would that be good?

Those who seek to stamp out stock market insider trading concede this point, so they object only when the knowledge is unavailable to the public. But the line between prohibited inside knowledge and permissible inside knowledge is far from clear. As law professor Daniel Fischel writes in Payback, although inside knowledge of specifics—an earnings report, a pending merger—is an illegal basis for stock market insider trading, more general inside knowledge is not.

Maybe the insider believes that a planned reorganization of a company's sales force is going better than expected or knows that a key executive is distracted by health or marital problems. Corporate insiders are permitted, even encouraged, to trade on this kind of informed hunch.

Why are stock transactions involving specific inside knowledge bad? The theory is that not only are the ignorant buyers and sellers taken advantage of, but—worse, perhaps—confidence in the securities markets themselves is sabotaged because potential participants, fearing they will be taken advantage of, will stay out of the market, depriving it of capital

This is a serious charge. What's the truth?

## Markets and Prices

A good place to start when inquiring whether an act is a crime is to ask: who's the victim? Current law has two in mind: the specific buyers or sellers of stock shares who did not possess the inside information and "the market."

Let's dispose of the second one first. "The market" cannot be a victim. It's an abstraction, not a living, breathing being. You can only victimize—that is, violate the rights of—individuals. But what about the claim that insider trading erodes confidence in the market? Even if that were true, it would not turn the act into a crime.

But the assumption that stock market insider trading erodes confidence in markets is false. On the contrary, confidence is increased by the realization that prices reflect up-to-date information. To explain this we must digress briefly to discuss the role of prices.

The price system does more than tell us what we must pay for goods and services. It produces information—in a highly concentrated and economic form—about supply and demand. We all use that information to guide our activities. For example, when a bad hurricane devastates a town and destroys homes, the new demand for plywood by suffering homeowners will bid up the price for the existing supply and attract new supply from other areas. (Unless socialistic laws prohibit "profiteering.") Whether or not I know about the new acute need for plywood, the higher prices will probably prompt me to postpone my plans to build a doghouse for Rover.

Note the social niceties of free pricing and the free movement of goods in response to price changes. Without making impossible interpersonal comparisons of subjective utility, most people would think that it's good that my doghouse will probably wait until after people rebuild their homes. The market's price system accomplishes this without a dictator issuing decrees or secret police shooting the uncooperative. Strangely, the market never gets credit from the intellectuals and "human rights" activists for this not inconsiderable achievement.

Of course, the contrast among most everyday alternatives is not so dramatic, but the principle is the same. The price system enables people to make decisions about scarce resources that take into account individual needs and knowledge spread throughout society, but without burdening them with an unmanageable amount of data.

Stock prices too are generated by supply and demand. But supply and demand for stocks are not disembodied concepts. They are generated, obviously enough, by suppliers and demanders—people with preferences, objectives, expectations, knowledge, and, therefore, plans. Part of what goes into an intention to buy or sell shares in a company is expectations about its future based on knowledge about its management, organization, and so on. These expectations are incorporated into the share price, and changes in expectations bring about changes in price. The more knowledgeable the participants, the more fully do prices perform their communications work. Nothing would undermine confidence in markets more than the belief that prices are out of date.

## The Martha Stewart Case and Stock Market Insider Trading

Look at Martha Stewart's ImClone stock sale. Regardless of what she knew, it is a fact that the Food and Drug Administration (FDA) was about to deny ImClone's application for the anti-cancer drug Erbitux. Obviously, the company and its stock would be worth more with FDA approval than without it.

Thus, in the time between the FDA's decision and its public announcement, ImClone's share price was unrealistically high. If shareholders with advance notice of the FDA's rejection sold their stock, they helped bring the price in line with the new set of facts.

The resulting price was a better price because it better reflected the revaluation. The direction of the price movement was also a signal to investors.

This leads to the question of whether particular buyers and sellers of stock are victims of insider trading. Again, let's look at the Stewart case, which is not about stock market insider trading but relies on the theory. No victim was named by the U.S. attorney. Stewart ordered her stock sold on December 27, 2001, after allegedly being told that the company's CEO was trying to sell his shares. (He was unable to sell them.) But she did not go out on the street, buttonhole a hapless pedestrian, and pitch the stock until he agreed to buy it. That's not how it works. She told her broker to sell, and the broker sold her shares to someone already looking to buy the stock.

This raises several interesting points. Anyone shopping for ImClone stock that day surely knew that a make-or-break decision from the FDA was due any time.

How can that buyer be described as a victim? Perhaps he wanted a long shot and was hedging with other stocks.

Or, since there was short-selling going on, he might have thought the stock would be a good deal in the longer run. (In fact, the stock price has come back because of a favorable Erbitux trial in Europe.)

Thus it is unlikely that a buyer of ImClone that day was naively shopping for stock. At any rate, for the government to assure the most clueless stock buyers that their knowledge is no worse than anyone else's in the market is to set them up for disappointment and to discourage the market research that any investor should engage in. No one is done any favors when insider trading is outlawed.

The upshot is that the buyers were not victims of Stewart.

By the way, on the day she sold, 7.7 million ImClone shares were traded—five times the volume of the day before. The members of then-CEO Sam Waksal's family who were tipped off early about the FDA sold only 150,000 shares. Maybe the knowledge wasn't so "inside" after all.

Note also that sellers of the stock were improving things for any unsophisticated buyers. If dumping their shares depressed the price, the buyers who would have bought anyway suffered a smaller loss than they would have had the stock not been dumped.

## Benefits of Stock Market Insider Trading

Of course, a naive stock speculator might decide after the fact that because he lacked inside information he bought or sold too soon, or didn't buy or sell at all. But that was a risk he should have been aware of going in. In contrast, the long-term stockholder, such as the proverbial "little old lady," who is not buying and selling in response to day-to-day price changes, is unlikely to be harmed by insider trading. On the contrary, this seller will most likely benefit.

"The long-term trend of stock prices is upward, so that, all other things being equal, occasions for good news should exceed those of bad," Henry Manne writes in *Insider Trading and the Stock Market*. "Any undeserved risk to investors resulting from insider trading must, therefore, constitute a very small fraction of the total risk assumed by long-term investors."

Manne points out that stock market insider trading is beneficial in another way. It's an appropriate method for corporations to compensate internal entrepreneurs for their work, because entrepreneurial insight is difficult to reward properly with bonuses or stock options. Fischel writes that insider trading (buying) can also be useful for letting executives "disclose" good news about the company without giving information away to competitors.

On the other hand, if stockholders dislike the practice, that will be reflected in lower stock prices for corporations that permit it. In the end, this is a matter for the competitive marketplace to sort out.

Stock Market Insider trading, of course, is a separate issue from the use of proprietary information in violation of a contractual duty. If Stewart's broker violated his duty to his other clients, they may have grounds for a civil suit and Merrill Lynch would have grounds to fire him. But it would be no cause for an SEC action or criminal indictment. The offense would be breach of contract, not stock market insider trading.

Viewpoint 4

> *"Some say there's a Wild West vibe to the crypto culture, and an element of mystery too."*

# Are Cryptocurrencies a Scam?

*Emma Fletcher*

*This viewpoint by Emma Fletcher takes a look at how scammers have used popular interest in cryptocurrencies to create new ways of defrauding investors. According to the Federal Trade Commission (FTC), a U.S. government agency that regulates trade, at one point investment scams had topped the list as the most lucrative ways to obtain cryptocurrency. But oftentimes, investors will discover that they've sent the cryptocurrency they bought directly into a scammer's wallet. In recent years, the number of cryptocurrency investment scams that have been reported have increased exponentially. Emma Fletcher is a senior data researcher at the FTC.*

As you read, consider the following questions:

1. How does this viewpoint say that scammers are taking advantage of the hype around cryptocurrencies?
2. What are some of the scams that this viewpoint identifies?
3. Who do these scams target?

"Cryptocurrency Buzz Drives Record Investment Scam Losses," by Emma Fletcher, Federal Trade Commission, May 17, 2021.

Investing in cryptocurrency means taking on risks, but getting scammed shouldn't be one of them. Reports to the FTC's Consumer Sentinel[1] suggest scammers are cashing in on the buzz around cryptocurrency and luring people into bogus investment opportunities in record numbers. Since October 2020, reports have skyrocketed, with nearly 7,000 people reporting losses of more than $80 million on these scams.[2] Their reported median loss? $1,900. Compared to the same period a year earlier, that's about twelve times the number of reports and nearly 1,000% more in reported losses.[3]

Some say there's a Wild West vibe to the crypto culture, and an element of mystery too. Cryptocurrency enthusiasts congregate online to chat about their shared passion. And with bitcoin's value soaring in recent months, new investors may be eager to get in on the action. All of this plays right into the hands of scammers. They blend into the scene with claims that can seem plausible because cryptocurrency is unknown territory for many people. Online, people may appear to be friendly and willing to share their "tips." But that can also be part of the ruse to get people to invest in their scheme. In fact, some of these schemes are based on referral chains, and work by bringing in people who then recruit new "investors."

Many people have reported being lured to websites that look like opportunities for investing in or mining cryptocurrencies, but are bogus. They often offer several investment tiers—the more you put in, the bigger the supposed return. Sites use fake testimonials and cryptocurrency jargon to appear credible, but promises of enormous, guaranteed returns are simply lies. These websites may even make it look like your investment is growing. But people report that, when they try to withdraw supposed profits, they are told to send even more crypto—and end up getting nothing back.

Then, there are "giveaway scams," supposedly sponsored by celebrities or other known figures in the cryptocurrency space, that promise to immediately multiply the cryptocurrency you send. But, people report that they discovered later that they'd simply sent their crypto directly to a scammer's wallet. For example, people have reported sending more than $2 million in cryptocurrency to Elon Musk impersonators over just the past six months.

Scammers even use online dating to draw people into cryptocurrency investment scams. Many people have reported believing they were in a long-distance relationship when their new love started chatting about a hot cryptocurrency opportunity, which they then acted on. About 20% of the money people reported losing through romance scams since October 2020 was sent in cryptocurrency, and many of these reports were from people who said they thought they were investing.[4]

Since October 2020, people ages 20 to 49 were over five times more likely to report losing money on cryptocurrency investment scams than older age groups.[5] The numbers are especially striking for people in their 20s and 30s: this group reported losing far more money on investment scams than on any other type of fraud,[6] and more than half of their reported investment scam losses were in cryptocurrency.[7] In contrast, people 50 and older were far less likely to report losing money on cryptocurrency investment scams. But when this group did lose money on these scams, their reported individual losses were higher, with a median reported loss of $3,250.

To be clear, while investment scams top the list as the most lucrative way to obtain cryptocurrency, scammers will use whatever story works to get people to send crypto. That often involves impersonating a government authority or a well-known business. For example, many people have told the FTC they loaded cash into Bitcoin ATM machines to pay imposters claiming to be from the Social Security Administration. Others reported losing money to scammers posing as Coinbase, a well-known cryptocurrency exchange. In fact, 14% of reported losses to imposters of all types are now in cryptocurrency.[8]

Here are some things to know to play it safe(er) when it comes to cryptocurrency:

- Promises of guaranteed huge returns or claims that your cryptocurrency will be multiplied are always scams.

- The cryptocurrency itself is the investment. You make money if you're lucky enough to sell it for more than you paid. Period. Don't trust people who say they know a better way.
- If a caller, love interest, organization, or anyone else insists on cryptocurrency, you can bet it's a scam.

To learn more about cryptocurrency scams, visit ftc.gov/cryptocurrency. If you spot a scam, report it to the FTC at ReportFraud.ftc.gov.

## Notes

1. This Spotlight is based on reports from consumers to the FTC or to any Consumer Sentinel Network data contributor.
2. This figure is based on 6,792 cryptocurrency investment scam reports submitted from October 1, 2020 through March 31, 2021. Cryptocurrency investment scam reports here and throughout this Spotlight are defined as reports categorized as investment related fraud that indicate cryptocurrency as the payment method. The investment related fraud category includes the following fraud subcategories: art, gems and rare coin investments, investment seminars and advice, stocks and commodity futures trading, and miscellaneous investments. About 92% of cryptocurrency investment scam reports from October 1, 2020 through March 31, 2021 are classified as miscellaneous investments.
3. From October 1 2019 through March 31, 2020, people submitted 570 cryptocurrency investment scam reports indicating $7.5 million in total losses.
4. This figure is based reports submitted from October 1, 2020 through March 31, 2021 that were classified as romance scams. Reports that did not specify a payment method are excluded. Of these, 1,147 reports totaling $35 million in reported losses indicated cryptocurrency as the payment method. These reports are distinct from reports classified as investment related fraud, with no overlap between the two.
5. About 86% of cryptocurrency investment related fraud reports submitted from October 1, 2020 through March 31, 2021 included age information. This age comparison is normalized based on the number of loss reports per million population by age during this period. Population numbers were obtained from the U.S. Census Bureau Annual Estimates of the Resident Population for Selected Age Groups by Sex for the United States (June 2020).
6. This ranking is based on a comparison of Sentinel fraud subcategories. From October 1, 2020 through March 31, 2021, consumers ages 20-39 reported $114 million in total losses on frauds classified as miscellaneous investments. Excluding unspecified reports, the subcategory with second highest reported losses by this age group was online shopping with $64 million in reported losses. These figures are not limited to reports indicating cryptocurrency as the payment method.
7. This figure is based on reports submitted from October 1, 2020 through March 31, 2021 that were categorized as investment related fraud and indicated a consumer age of range of 20 to 39. Reports that did not specify a payment method are

excluded. Of these, 3,581 reports totaling $35 million in reported losses indicated cryptocurrency as the payment method.

8. This figure is based on reports from October 1, 2020 through March 31, 2021 that were categorized as imposter scams. Reports that did not specify a payment method are excluded. Of these, 3,494 reports totaling $64 million in reported losses indicated cryptocurrency as the payment method. The imposter scams category includes the following fraud subcategories: business imposters, family and friend imposters, government imposters, romance scams, and tech support scams.

VIEWPOINT

*"Unlike banks, life insurance companies, casinos, currency exchangers, and even precious-metals dealers, auction houses and art sellers have no obligation to report large cash transactions to a governing authority."*

# The Risks of Investing in Art

***International Monetary Fund***

*This viewpoint examines how the largely unregulated art market—similar to the largely unregulated market for cryptocurrency—can attract scammers. In particular, the author looks at how the loopholes in how the marketplace is regulated allow money launderers to use art galleries as a way to make their money appear as though it's from a legitimate source. In particular, the viewpoint considers how galleries aid money laundering schemes and the ways that authorities try to crack down on them. The International Monetary Fund is the primary financial agency run by the United Nations.*

As you read, consider the following questions:

1. How can art dealing operate as a vehicle for fraud?
2. Why does this viewpoint suggest that interest in cracking down on illicit art and antiquities deals is growing?

"The Loosely Regulated Art Market Is Rife with Opportunities for Washing Illicit Cash," International Monetary Fund. Reprinted by permission.

3. What are some of the ways this viewpoint suggests combatting fraud in the art world?

Matthew Green was raised in the heady world of fine arts, surrounded from boyhood by the works of Old Masters and Impressionists. His father, Richard, the owner of two of London's most illustrious galleries, dealt in legendary names like Picasso, Constable, Chagall, and Brueghel. Matthew Green, 51, was preparing to take over the family business so his father could pursue new passions.

But in late 2017, US prosecutors say, Green fell in with the owners of a Mauritius-based investment company, Beaufort Securities, that engaged in fraud, stock manipulation, and money laundering. For Beaufort's owners, duping investors into buying worthless securities was the easy part. The hard part was making the ill-gotten profit appear legitimate to regulators. Beaufort had done so in the past by depositing money under false names in offshore banks, then slipping it into the global banking system little by little. The company had also used the time-tested trick of buying real estate and quickly selling it off, often at a loss, to convert illegal proceeds into assets that could be accounted for as the fruit of a property deal.

Now, money launderers like Beaufort were searching for less obvious ways to scrub their cash, and Matthew Green knew how to trade in multimillion-dollar works of art. Approached in late 2017 by the Beaufort conspirators—one of whom was in fact an undercover US federal agent who had infiltrated Beaufort—Green allegedly said he would accept £6.7 million (about $9 million at the time) in what he knew to be the yield of securities fraud in exchange for a 1965 Picasso, *Personnages*. Green would draw up phony ownership papers saying the work had been sold, all the while keeping the Picasso stored away. Down the road he would pretend to buy it back from his coconspirators at a lower price, keeping 5 to 10 percent of the laundered cash for himself.

"Art is a very attractive vehicle to launder money," says Peter D. Hardy, a former US prosecutor who now advises corporations and industries on compliance with anti-money-laundering requirements. "It can be hidden or smuggled, transactions often are private, and prices can be subjective and manipulated—and extremely high."

After a slew of recent cases in the United States and Europe, the momentum toward a crackdown on illicit art and antiquities deals is growing. The legitimate art market is itself enormous—estimated at $67.4 billion worldwide at the end of 2018. According to the United Nations Office on Drugs and Crime, the underground art market, which includes thefts, fakes, illegal imports, and organized looting, may bring in as much as $6 billion annually. The portion attributed to money laundering and other financial crimes is in the $3 billion range.

For Green, dabbling in the dark art of money laundering has ended poorly. He has been indicted in the United States on six counts of attempted money laundering, and his gallery in the Mayfair district of London has been declared insolvent by British regulators. Although Green has not been identified as a fugitive, court records indicate that US prosecutors have disclosed his indictment and arrest warrant to law enforcement agencies in the United Kingdom, Hungary, Saint Vincent and the Grenadines, and Mauritius. He has also been ordered to surrender the Picasso.

The tactics used by Green and the others charged in the Picasso scheme remain easy to replicate, at least for now. Green was taking advantage of a regulatory loophole that US and European legislators are working hard to close. Unlike banks, life insurance companies, casinos, currency exchangers, and even precious-metals dealers, auction houses and art sellers have no obligation to report large cash transactions to a governing authority. In fact, dealers can keep the names of buyers and sellers anonymous. And unlike US businesses that deal in large sums of money, they do not have to file so-called suspicious activity reports with the US Treasury

Department if they have doubts about the origins of the money they are being paid.

## Bill in Congress

Under the Illicit Art and Antiquities Trafficking Prevention Act under consideration in Congress, the US government would require "dealers in art and antiquities" to establish anti-money-laundering programs, keep records of cash purchases, and report suspicious activity and transactions exceeding $10,000 to federal regulators. In addition, the art industry would be required to look into a client's background and examine purchases and sales for evidence that the money might be tainted.

In the European Union, under its Fifth Anti-Money Laundering Directive, art businesses would be obliged to augment efforts to vet customers and to discern "as far as reasonably possible" the purpose of all large, unusually complex, or secretive transactions.

In the view of many art dealers, the legal changes in both the United States and the European Union would strip the vendors of a major selling point—the ability to offer anonymity to clients and preserve the opacity of the art market. In years past, when the fine arts market was seen as a more genteel pursuit, there was no real inclination by the authorities to police it as strenuously as the banking or brokerage trades. All that has changed in the past decade or so because of the enormous amounts of money pouring into art collecting and the growing focus on stymieing the clandestine trafficking in looted and smuggled artifacts from war-torn nations.

Law enforcement officials and even some art merchants now say that excessive secrecy has become a drawback because more and more money launderers have discovered that the art market can be used as an easy conduit. As noted by the FBI and Interpol, "in comparison with other trade sectors, the art market faces a higher risk of exposure to dubious financial practices" because "the volume of legally questionable transactions is noticeably higher than in other global markets."

The indictment filed against Matthew Green and his confederates even recounts a conversation, tape-recorded by an undercover agent, in which Green allegedly crows that "the art trade is the only market that is this unregulated." A client "could even buy the art under a false name with no repercussions," Green is quoted as saying.

"More cases involving artwork and money laundering undoubtedly would be uncovered by law enforcement if art and antiquities dealers were added to the list of businesses legally liable for reporting suspect payments," says Rick St. Hilaire, a former US prosecutor and an expert on art and antiquities law. "For now, it's wide open."

Supporters of expanded regulation say all they want is for the trade in fine art, cultural property, and ancient artifacts to be subjected to the same financial regulations that banks and other industries face.

"The art market is an ideal playing ground for money laundering," says Thomas Christ, a board member of the Basel Institute on Governance, a Swiss nonprofit that has proposed anti-money-laundering standards for art market operators. He added, "We have to ask for clear transparency, where you got the money from and where it is going."

## The Industry Objects

Not surprisingly, the art industry is fighting the regulations. Some sectors are asserting that examples of actual money laundering via the art trade are rare or exaggerated by law enforcement agencies eager to generate sensational headlines. Others, like the International Confederation of Art and Antique Dealers Associations, say the reporting requirements are too burdensome for smaller players in the art market.

At a conference on money laundering last year, James McAndrew, a former Department of Homeland Security special agent who now lobbies on behalf of dealers and collectors, said that "there has not been an art dealer or collector convicted for laundering money through art. The idea that auctions are nefarious or evil is outrageous because it hasn't been proven." Peter Tompa, director of the Global Heritage Alliance, which advocates for collectors, museums and the trade in archaeological objects, warned that many in the trade would exit the market because the new standards would be too costly to adopt.

And the Committee for Cultural Policy, an art and antiquities think tank, said that "it is not practical to use art to launder money, especially antiques and antiquities, because art sells slowly, and buyers are usually collectors," not criminals seeking a quick deal to "legitimize" dubious money.

But advocates say the stratospheric valuations placed on artworks by even second-tier artists leave them no choice but to impose constraints on a vulnerable industry at a time when drug kingpins, oil oligarchs, and assorted kleptocrats are desperate to turn their dirty money into a clean or fungible asset. For now, the momentum is with them, and there are enough money laundering prosecutions to justify those concerns.

A 2014 case known as *U.S. v. Ronald Belciano et al.*, for example, involved both the distribution of marijuana and a conspiracy to launder the profits using artwork. Police seized over $4 million in cash and confiscated approximately 125 pounds of marijuana and 33 paintings worth more than $619,000 from a storage warehouse in Pennsylvania. Prosecutors said the drug dealers had accepted the artworks in lieu of cash after being promised that they could sell them back for laundered money once the art dealers had buried the transactions in their books. In 2015, Belciano was sentenced to five years in prison.

In another high-profile case, a Brazilian financier was accused of embezzling millions from his bank and trying to launder the money by acquiring expensive art, including Jean-Michel Basquiat's *Hannibal* (1981). According to federal prosecutors in New York, the financier, Edemar Cid Ferreira, tried to smuggle the Basquiat and about 90 other high-value works of art into the United States using papers that declared the value of each object at $100. Even though he was convicted and sentenced to 21 years in 2006, appeals and complexities in the legal system meant the United States could not repatriate the works to Brazil until 2017.

And small-scale scams occur every day. Indian officials, for example, say antiquities looted from remote temples and tombs are used as a means of currency exchange. The items are shipped to dealers in Hong Kong SAR or Bangkok—often falsely listed in manifests as replicas worth a few rupees. Collectors and traders are standing by to pay thousands of dollars for the relics, which come with fake documents attesting to their legal purchase. The dealers keep a share of the take and filter the rest of the money back to crime rings in India through unregulated nonbank financial companies.

Deborah Lehr, chairman of the Antiquities Coalition, a Washington, DC–based organization fighting trafficking in artifacts, warns that terrorist groups are already using the art and antiquities industry to raise money by plundering ancient cultural sites and employing intermediaries to sell off the looted goods. "A key priority is shutting the US market to illicit antiquities while encouraging responsible trade practices," she says.

Given that upward of 70 to 90 percent of auction catalog listings for valuable antiquities provide scant information about the seller, art merchants would be wise to accept the inevitable and move toward greater transparency and more due diligence, says Hardy, the former prosecutor. The proposed regulations, he says, would simply enshrine into law the steps that art dealers ought to be taking in the first place to stave off criminal acts.

"Sometimes," he says, "the provenance of the funds can be more critical than the provenance of the art."

> *"Fraudsters use different means, including through promotional videos, social media, email, phone conversations, and in-person meetings, to lure victims into scams. If it seems too good to be true, it probably is."*

## How to Avoid Investment Scams

***U.S. Securities and Exchange Commission***

*In this viewpoint, the U.S. Securities and Exchange Commission (SEC) explains some of the common tricks con artists use to lure investors into scams. Some of these tricks include "get rich quick and easily" schemes, which are among the most common types of scams. Other tactics con artists use include creating a sense of urgency around the fake investment opportunity and collecting fake testimonials from alleged investors. By being aware of the tricks used in fraudulent investment opportunities, the SEC argues that investors can avoid falling for these scams. The U.S. Securities and Exchange Commission is an agency of the U.S. government that enforces the law against market manipulation.*

As you read, consider the following questions:

1. What two steps does the SEC suggest can help prevent you from falling for an investment scam?

"Don't Fall for an Investment Scam—Investor Alert," The U.S. Securities and Exchange Commission, October 10, 2019.

2. How do con artists create a sense of urgency?
3. According to this viewpoint, why aren't testimonials dependable?

The SEC's Office of Investor Education and Advocacy (OIEA) and Retail Strategy Task Force (RSTF) want Main Street investors to be aware of tactics fraudsters use to lure investors into scams.

Two simple steps can help protect you from being swindled in an investment scam:

- **Check the background of anyone selling or offering you an investment and confirm that the person is currently registered or licensed.** It only takes a few minutes using the free and simple search tools on Investor.gov. Before you hand over any money or share your contact information, verify that the person is currently registered or licensed and find out if he or she has a disciplinary history. Investors can also use SALI to find information about certain people who have had judgments or orders issued against them in SEC court actions or administrative proceedings.
- **Look out for common tricks that con artists use to attract investors.** Fraudsters use different means, including through promotional videos, social media, email, phone conversations, and in-person meetings, to lure victims into scams. If it seems too good to be true, it probably is. Here are a few examples of actual videos used to cheat investors out of millions of dollars (as alleged in *SEC v. Atkinson* and *SEC v. Montano*):
- **Get Rich Quickly and Easily.** One of the most common gimmicks con artists use is to promise investors that they will make a lot of money in a short period of time – that they will "get rich quick." Con artists may trick investors into believing that they will make tons of money with little or no effort (for example, for purchasing products or for performing

trivial tasks, such as clicking on digital ads each day). This tactic often uses images of lavish lifestyles and luxury items to create the illusion of future riches (for example, wealth, fancy cars, mansions, yachts, vacations, etc.).

- In *SEC v. Senderov and Babazara*, the SEC took action against a fraudulent multi-million dollar scheme that used boiler-room-like call centers to solicit investors. The SEC alleges that the call centers' employees had a business practice of promising investors that the investments offered would be highly profitable. Examples of these promises allegedly include employees telling investors: (1) "We will watch your money double in the next 30 days with no further investments"; (2) if you deposit $30,000 to $40,000, you can expect profits of $3,000 to $4,000 per month; and (3) the goal is for your investments to earn 7 percent per month. According to the SEC's complaint, many investors lost a significant portion of the money they invested.
- **Urgency.** Con artists often claim an investment opportunity will be gone tomorrow. They create a false sense of urgency so investors turn over money "right now," without researching the investment. They may trick investors into believing that the investment "opportunity" is limited to a certain number of investors who can get in on it or has a deadline triggered by an event that will soon occur. Some promotional videos may impose a deadline or feature a fake countdown (for example, "only 12 spots left…11…10…9….").
- In *SEC v. Petersen*, the SEC brought charges against the owners and operators of several boiler-room-like call centers for defrauding investors. The SEC's complaint alleges the call centers' employees passed themselves off as "brokers" and "financial advisors" despite having little or no relevant experience. These so-called "brokers" and "financial advisors" allegedly also tried to trick investors into making additional and often large deposits by creating a false sense of urgency. The SEC alleges that the defendants' training materials stated

that "you need to create urgency at the beginning of the call" and defined "urgency" as "giving the client a reason to proceed today and not tomorrow." According to the SEC's complaint, the so-called "brokers" and "financial advisors" created this "urgency" by telling investors about supposed imminent market events that created profitable trading opportunities but only if the investor acted immediately. The defendants' alleged high-pressure sales tactics included citing upcoming earnings announcements by well-known public companies or expected public disclosures of economic news (for example, the jobless rate) to trick investors to invest more money.

- **Fake Testimonials.** Con artists may pay people to post fake online reviews or appear in videos falsely claiming to have gotten rich from some investment opportunity. Even testimonials that appear to be independent and unbiased reviews – for example on a website purporting to "review" products and investment opportunities – may be part of the scam.

Never rely solely on testimonials in making an investment decision. Also, depictions of skyrocketing investment accounts often are fake. The potential for high investment returns usually involves high risk. Promises of high investment returns, with little or no risk, are classic warning signs of fraud.

Don't be hoodwinked if someone tries to use these lines on you. If you suspect that someone is trying to rip you off with an investment scam, protect yourself and others – report it to the SEC.

## Periodical and Internet Sources Bibliography

*The following articles have been selected to supplement the diverse views presented in this chapter.*


Daniel Akst, "The Original Ponzi Schemer," *Wall Street Journal*, October 15, 2020. https://www.wsj.com/articles/the-original-ponzi-schemer-11602778470.

Rebecca Ballhaus, Brody Mullins, Chad Day, John West, Joe Palazzolo, and James V. Grimaldi, "Federal Officials Trade Stock in Companies Their Agencies Oversee," *Wall Street Journal*, October 11, 2022. https://www.wsj.com/articles/government-officials-invest-in-companies-their-agencies-oversee-11665489653.

Russell Berman, "The Bill That Congress Might Be Embarrassed Enough to Pass," the *Atlantic*, January 30, 2022. https://www.theatlantic.com/politics/archive/2022/01/congress-stock-trading-ban/621402/.

Matthew Goldstein, Alexandra Stevenson, Maureen Farrell and David Yaffe-Bellany, "How FTX's Sister Firm Brought the Crypto Exchange Down," *New York Times*, November 18, 2022. https://www.nytimes.com/2022/11/18/business/ftx-alameda-ties.html

Matt Levine, "Insiders Are Good at Trading" *Bloomberg*, September 29, 2021. https://www.bloomberg.com/opinion/articles/2021-09-29/insiders-are-good-at-trading.

Tom McGinty and Mark Maremont, "CEO Stock Sales Raise Questions About Insider Trading," *Wall Street Journal*, June 29, 2022. https://www.wsj.com/articles/executive-stock-sales-questions-insider-trading-11656514551.

Patrick Radden Keefe, "Making Insider Trading Legal," *New Yorker*, October 27, 2015. https://www.newyorker.com/business/currency/making-insider-trading-legal.

Tom Schoenberg and Matt Robinson, "US Probes Insider Trading in Prearranged Executive Stock Sales," *Bloomberg*, November 3, 2022. https://www.bloomberg.com/news/articles/2022-11-03/us-probes-insider-trading-in-prearranged-executive-stock-sales.

David Segal, "The Crypto Ponzi Scheme Avenger," *New York Times*, November 11, 2022. https://www.nytimes.com/2022/11/11/business/crypto-ponzi-scheme-hyperfund.html.

Paul Sullivan, "A Bigger Risk Than GameStop? Beware the Ponzi Scheme Next Door," *New York Times,* April 14, 2021. https://www.nytimes.com/2021/02/05/your-money/ponzi-schemes-stock-market.html.

# For Further Discussion

## Chapter 1

1. What are some of the main negative impacts of political corruption, according to the viewpoint by Elvin Mirzayev?
2. According to the viewpoints in this chapter, what are some of the negative effects of corruption on various aspects of society?
3. Why are the authors of the viewpoints from Transform! Europe and Brasilwire skeptical of the motivations behind a major anticorruption probe in Brazil?

## Chapter 2

1. According to the viewpoint from Jagran Josh, why do police generally go after money laundering instead of the crimes it's meant to conceal?
2. What does Brian Monroe say appeals to banks about dealing in laundered money?
3. What reason does Mark Hudspeth give for why money laundering operations are deliberately complicated?

## Chapter 3

1. What does Todd Pickles say is behind the U.S. government's "China Initiative?"
2. According to the viewpoints in this chapter, how is trade secret theft investigated and prosecuted?
3. After reading the viewpoint by Charles Duhigg, how do you think he believes trade secret laws should be reformed?

## Chapter 4

1. Why does Adams Hayes think that Bernie Madoff was never caught until he ran out money?
2 Does Andrew Sabastian ultimately think insider trading is good or bad for markets? Explain your reasoning.
3. Why does Emma Fletcher argue that new technologies like cryptocurrencies are particularly susceptible to fraud?

# Organizations to Contact

*The editors have compiled the following list of organizations concerned with the issues debated in this book. The descriptions are derived from materials provided by the organizations. All have publications or information available for interested readers. The list was compiled on the date of publication of the present volume; the information provided here may change. Be aware that many organizations take several weeks or longer to respond to inquiries, so allow as much time as possible.*

### Anti-Corruption Agencies Strengthening Initiative

Alt-Moabit 96
10559 Berlin, Germany
+49 30 3438 200
email: ti@transparency.org
website: transparency.org/en/projects/anti-corruption-agency-strengthening-initiative

Part of the German group Transparency International, the Anti-Corruption Agencies Strengthening Initiative works with anti-corruption agencies around the world "to strengthen their effectiveness." The group does this by making various biennial assessments of those agencies and encouraging governments to invest in stronger oversight and enforcement mechanisms.

### The Anti-Corruption Working Group

685 3rd Ave.
New York, NY 10017
(212) 907-1301
email: jamili@unglobalcompact.org
website: unglobalcompact.org/take-action/action/anti-corruption-working-group

A part of the United Nations Global Compact, its Anti-Corruption Working Group is a multi-stakeholder group that issues cross-sectoral and collaborative efforts in aid of ending corruption around the world. Among its accomplishments has been to mobilize companies around the review mechanism of the UN Convention against Corruption.

**Association of Certified Fraud Examiners (ACFE)**

The Gregor Building
716 West Ave.
Austin, TX 78701
(800) 245-3321
email: MemberServices@ACFE.com
website: www.acfe.com

The ACFE bills itself as the world's largest anti-fraud organization and provides certifications on fraud examining to people with a professional interest in the subject. Since it was founded in 1985, the group has grown to certify over 90,000 experts in uncovering and reducing white collar fraud.

**The Center for Advanced Defense Studies**

1201 I Street Northwest, Suite 200
Washington, DC 20005
(202) 289-3332
email: info@c4ads.org
website: https://c4ads.org

The Center for Advanced Defense Studies is a nonprofit research organization that provides data-driven analysis that's used to detect and disrupt illicit networks around the world. Some of the programs the group runs target "Organized Crime and Grand Corruption" and "Conflict Finance and Irregular Threats," the latter including financial drivers of conflict.

## Coalition for Integrity

1100 13th Street, NW, 8th Floor
Washington, DC 20005
(202) 589-1616
email: administration@coalitionforintegrity.org
website: www.coalitionforintegrity.org

The Coalition for Integrity is a nonprofit group that tasks itself with promoting integrity and combating corruption in the public and private sectors. Among its ways of doing this are publishing guidance reports to assist companies in adopting clear anti-corruption policies and effective anti-corruption procedures, as well as hosting private-sector roundtables on business integrity, anti-corruption compliance issues, and best practices.

## The Division of Law Enforcement's White Collar Investigation Team

Attorney General's Office
California Department of Justice
Attn: Public Inquiry Unit
P.O. Box 944255
Sacramento, CA 94244-2550
(916) 210-6276
website: oag.ca.gov/bi/wcit

A division of the California Department of Justice, the White Collar Investigation Team is tasked with investigating white collar crimes, such as major fraud, theft by false pretense, money laundering, corporate fraud, securities and commodities fraud, mortgage fraud, financial institution fraud, bank fraud and embezzlement, fraud against the government, mass marketing fraud, and health care fraud. While the team works on crimes that take place in California, they also operate in other states and regions that impact Californians.

### The Human Rights Foundation's Anti-Corruption Initiative

350 5th Ave #4202
New York, NY 10118
(212) 246-8486
email: contact@hrf.org
website: https://hrf.org/anti-corruption-initiative

Run by the nonprofit Human Rights Foundation, its recent Anti-Corruption Initiative focuses on documenting the links between corruption, authoritarianism, and human rights abuses. The group does this by publicizing instances where "kleptocratic regimes are aided and abetted by oligarchs and their cronies inside democratic nations abroad," according to their website.

### The International Anti-Corruption Coordination Centre (IACCC)

Units 1–6 Citadel Place
Tinworth Street
London SE11 5EF
0370 496 7622
email: communication@nca.gov.uk
website: www.nationalcrimeagency.gov.uk/what-we-do/crime-threats/bribery-corruption-and-sanctions-evasion/international-anti-corruption-centre

A division of the United Kingdom's National Crime Agency, the IACCC brings together various specialist law enforcement officers from multiple agencies around the world to tackle allegations of corruption on a large scale. The crimes that this group focuses on include bribery of public officials, embezzlement, and the laundering of the proceeds of crime.

### International Association of Anti-Corruption Authorities (IAACA)

ICAC Building
303 Java Road
North Point
Hong Kong, China
+852 28263361
email: info@iaaca.net
website: www.iaaca.net

Based in Hong Kong, the IAACA is a non-political anticorruption organization that promotes the effective implementation of the United Nations Convention against Corruption. Since its establishment in 2006, the group has held numerous annual conferences and general meetings, as well as anti-corruption training events.

### The National White Collar Crime Center

4905 Dickens Road Suite 106
Richmond, VA 23230-1953
(804) 273-6932
email: contact@nw3c.org
website: www.nw3c.org

The National White Collar Crime Center runs a nationwide support system for law enforcement and regulatory agencies that deal with the prevention, investigation, and prosecution of economic and high-tech crime. The group's support includes training on various cybercrimes, economic crime, intelligence analysis, digital forensics, and intellectual property crime.

### Organized Crime and Corruption Reporting Project (OCCRP)

1220 L St. NW, Ste. 100 497
Washington, DC 20005
(202) 470-3510
email: info@occrp.org
website: www.occrp.org

The OCCRP is a global network of investigative journalists that report on issues like corruption and other white collar crimes. Among its accomplishments has been breaking news of the largest tax fraud in Russian history, breaking a $1 billion bribery ring involving the telecom giant TeliaSonera and reporting on a massive money laundering scheme called the Russian Laundromat, which moved tens of billions of dollars into Europe using offshore companies.

# Bibliography of Books

Ken Bensinger, *Red Card: FIFA and the Fall of the Most Powerful Men in Sports*. New York, NY: Profile Books, 2018.

Jake Bernstein, *Secrecy World: Inside the Panama Papers Investigation of Illicit Money Networks and the Global Elite*, New York, NY: Henry Holt & Company, 2017.

Eliot Brown and Maureen Farrell, *The Cult of We: WeWork, Adam Neumann, and the Great Startup Delusion*. New York, NY: Crown Publishing, 2021.

Tom Burgis, *Kleptopia: How Dirty Money is Conquering the World*. New York, NY: Harper, 2020.

John Carreyrou. *Bad Blood: Secrets and Lies in a Silicon Valley Startup*. New York, NY: Knopf Publishing, 2018.

Dan Davies, *Lying for Money: How Legendary Frauds Reveal the Workings of Our World*. New York, NY: Scribner, 2021.

Diana B. Henriques, *The Wizard of Lies: Bernie Madoff and the Death of Trust*. New York, NY: St. Martin's Griffin, 2017.

Thomas Levenson, *Money for Nothing: The Scientists, Fraudsters, and Corrupt Politicians Who Reinvented Money, Panicked a Nation, and Made the World Rich*. New York, NY: Penguin Random House, 2020.

Casey Michel, *American Kleptocracy: How the U.S. Created the World's Greatest Money Laundering Scheme in History*. New York, NY: St. Martin's Press, 2021.

Bastian Obermayer and Frederik Obermaier, *The Panama Papers: Breaking the Story of How the Rich and Powerful Hide Their Money*. London, UK: Oneworld Publications, 2016.

Desmond Shum, *Red Roulette: An Insider's Story of Wealth, Power, Corruption and Vengeance in Today's China*. New York, NY: Simon & Schuster, 2021.

Jennifer Taub, *Big Dirty Money: The Shocking Injustice and Unseen Cost of White Collar Crime*. New York NY: Viking, 2020.

Zephyr Teachout, *Corruption in America: From Benjamin Franklin's Snuff Box to Citizens United*. Cambridge, MA: Harvard University Press, 2014.

Tom Wright and Bradley Hope, *Billion Dollar Whale: The Man Who Fooled Wall Street, Hollywood, and the World*. New York NY: Hachette Books, 2018.

Eilene Zimmerman, *Smacked: A Story of White-Collar Ambition, Addiction, and Tragedy*. New York, NY: Random House, 2020.

# Index

## F



## G



## H



## I



## J



## L



## M

## N



## O



## P



## R



## S